EVIL AND EXILE

Evil and Exile

by

ELIE WIESEL

and

PHILIPPE-MICHAËL DE SAINT-CHERON

translated by

Jon Rothschild

UNIVERSITY OF NOTRE DAME PRESS
NOTRE DAME   LONDON

Library of Congress Cataloging-in-Publication Data

Wiesel, Elie, 1928–
    Evil and exile / by Elie Wiesel and Philippe de
Saint-Cheron; translated by Jon Rothschild.
        p. cm.
    Translations of French interviews.
    ISBN 0-268-00922-8
    1. Wiesel, Elie, 1928-   –Interviews.
    2. Authors, French–20th century–Interviews.
    3. Authors, American–20th century–
    Interviews. 4 Civilization, Modern–20th
    century. 5. Peace. I. Saint-Cheron,
    Philippe de. II. Title.
    PQ2683.I32Z463 1990
    813′ .54–dc20   89-40748
        L8867

To the memory of the little girl
of the Armero catastrophe in Colombia,
whose face, seen one night on television,
haunts us still.

For Deborah and Sarah.

Contents

Prologue

This book was born of love and veneration: love of the tradition, teachings, history, and living memory of Judaism; veneration of a man and his destiny, a writer and his work, both of which embody the very essence of the mystery of Israel's destruction and survival in our century.

It was thanks to Elie Wiesel (as well as Emmanuel Levinas and Claude Vigée) that I came to recognize the House of Israel as my own, the One God revealed to and in Israel as my God, and the history of this people, dispersed throughout the world yet united by a like aspiration, bearers of an eternal spirit, as my collective history. Elie Wiesel's was the first great Jewish voice I heard, and it was that voice that made me become anew what I had been by birth, albeit unknowingly: a child of Israel. It is therefore my hope that this book might be more than a mere collection of interviews like so many others, and that it might testify to the spiritual upheaval that led me, after nearly thirty years of Christian education and Christian faith, to embrace the Covenant of Abraham, Isaac, and Jacob.

The voice I heard through Elie Wiesel spoke to me in the words of Ruth: "Thy people shall be my people, and thy God my God." To which I would add: and thy memory shall be my memory. I had been unaware that this people, this God, and this memory were already mine, and it was Elie Wiesel's voice that revealed it to me.

1

Elie Wiesel is the herald of Jewish memory of the
Shoah. No one can hear his words and remain
unmoved.

Most of the interviews in this book were conducted
between June 23 and June 26, 1987, a week marked by
an important event: John Paul II's meeting at the Vatican
with Austrian President Kurt Waldheim. There is little
need to recall the indignation aroused by that meeting in
the international Jewish community and elsewhere. Elie
Wiesel protested publicly.

*   *   *

New York, Tuesday, June 23, 1987.

I decided to walk to Elie Wiesel's, crossing Central
Park from west to east. On the corner of Fifth Avenue
and 66th Street stands Temple Emmanu-el, the world's
largest synagogue, built in the Roman Byzantine style.
With its central nave, capable of accommodating twenty-
five hundred worshippers, its lateral nave, its organ, its
windows, and its tabernacle containing the Torah, deco-
rated with stars of David and flanked by menorahs on either side, this Jewish temple looks more like a cathedral
than a synagogue. On 62nd Street, just a few hundred
yards away, stands the far more classical Fifth Avenue
Synagogue. The proximity of these two temples, the one
reformed, the other traditional, is a reminder that the
Jewish community of New York is one of the world's
largest.

About ten minutes later, I arrived at the building
where Elie Wiesel lives. He had not yet returned, and I
had to wait.

I glanced once more at my list of questions, recalling
the autumn day in 1983 when I first met Elie Wiesel, at
the Hotel Port-Royal in Paris. Serena had been with me,
and I was terribly impressed that I was about to encounter a man who had survived hell and whose words had

moved me as no other's since Malraux. Here in New York, however, jet lag and the fatigue of my trip, combined with the many months of waiting, had created a mood of feverish unreality.

"Hello, Michael, how are you? How was the trip? Tiring?"

"This is the most beautiful day of my life," I replied. He smiled.

We went upstairs to the study in his apartment. I took a seat and quickly took out my questions, not wanting to waste his valuable time. We were surrounded by bookshelves; it was as though we had entered a kingdom of books, a Jewish kingdom. Indeed, books, and the Book, probably have a larger place in Jewish life than in the life of any other people. A few moments later Elie Wiesel sat down opposite me. He looked tired.

In books, as in life, the first question is always the most difficult. I was suddenly apprehensive, but I knew that without a question, there could be no answer. I had to begin.

Our entire dialogue was dominated by the two questions of Chance and Meaning. Are they irreconcilable by nature? How can Chance be reconciled with Faith?

Chance is the supreme question posed by the Shoah, whose unimaginable enormity forces us to rethink everything. On the night of his arrival in Birkenau, Elie Wiesel lost his mother and his younger sister, Tzipora. He witnessed the daily torment of his father, who was finally taken away to Buchenwald, where he died. How is it that Elie Wiesel survived? He raises the question himself in *A Jew Today*: "Birkenau, Auschwitz, Monowitz-Buna, Buchenwald: that very first night I might have joined the procession of old men and children. I might have remained in one camp and not reached the next. I might have passed through all four and followed my father into icy nothingness before the end of the night. Liberated by the American army, ravaged by poisoned blood, I might have succumbed on a hospital bed, a free man. After being reunited with my comrades, I might have missed the children's transport leaving for France; I might have gone back to Transylvania or elsewhere, done other things. I might have engaged in or endured other battles. I might not have lived the story of my life. Nor written it."

But the question remains: Was it Chance or Miracle? His answer is chilling: it was pure chance.

Elie Wiesel speaks a truth that brooks no facile consolation. All his work is stamped by the twofold mystery of the silence of God and of man, mysteries that are joined in the further enigma of God's encounter with man. His work, however, is novelistic rather than philosophical; it is part of the religious tradition of Hasidism, the movement of Jewish mysticism born in central Europe in the eighteenth century.

Above all else, Elie Wiesel aspires to be a *witness*, linking memory to the present, testifying against forgetfulness, but also against a dangerous proliferation of words. And witness is the translation of the Greek word *martyr*.

First Day

Why should we be surprised that murderers wreak death among those who preserve the Torah of Life? How else to acknowledge the Evil in evil and the Death in death? How else to prevent facile theodicies, gratuitous consolation, and painless compassion? How else to acknowledge the insensate meaning of the mystery of death?

Emmanuel Levinas
Noms propres

Evil

Philippe de Saint-Cheron: *Earlier this year you were awarded an honorary doctorate at the Sorbonne. During your address you recalled that as a child, when you came home from the heder, your mother would always ask, "Did you have a good question for your Masters today?"*

I wonder if you might do me the honor of letting me act as your pupil for these few days, and I hope that my questions will not be too unworthy of the honor you have granted me.

In a certain sense, to agree to do a book of questions and answers amounts to breaking silence. The very act of allowing me to elicit your thoughts, wisdom, and experience on the subject of Evil and Exile itself raises the question of speech and silence, does it not?

Elie Wiesel: Everything raises the question of speech and silence. Whether we speak or remain silent is always matter of a choice. The problem is not to choose between speech and silence, but to try to make sure that speech does not become the enemy of silence and that silence does not become a betrayal of speech. We must strive for a deep inner harmony between the two, such that each becomes a complement and extension of the other, and sometimes its very meaning as well.

You use speech, yet at the same time you are against . . .

But that's the way it is: to be against speech one must use it. The man who keeps silent is not really against speech; he has simply chosen silence. To be against it, one would have to say openly: I am against speech. Speech alone can take a stand against speech.

Why is it that you are alive today while others are not? In other words, what accounts for your survival? Do you think it was providence, predestination, miracle, or simply chance?

It would frighten me to use the word "miracle" to describe the fact that others suffered so much more than I did. To say that my presence here is the result of a miracle would be to say that millions of others did not benefit from any miracle. The word "miracle" would then be an accusation: why weren't my many friends, comrades, and companions saved by a miracle, not to mention all the others unknown to me? No, I prefer to think that it was pure chance, and indeed that is what it was. I did not do anything to survive. When I think about it, that's how I remember it. I never took any particular step, never made any definite decision or thought of any way out. It was pure chance.

It was in Signes d'exode *that you first recounted an event that touched you very deeply, one linked to your memory of your mother. The last time you saw your master, the rabbi of Wizhnitz, he told her, "Someday your son will be a person we can both be proud of, but neither of us will live to see it."*
Were you destined for greatness?

He was a very wise man indeed, and those were seething times—1935 and 1936, days of impending ordeals. For a man like him, capable of comparing past and present and of drawing conclusions about the future, it was almost a matter of logic.

Still, he had a stunning gift of foresight.

I wouldn't say that. I think he was just trying to console my mother. It was his way of giving her son his blessing. I don't like to look for miracles. The word is too strong. He was trying to reassure my mother, that's all.

How do you reconcile the ideas of providence and silence, or what Buber called the eclipse of God? Do you feel that providence died during the Shoah? What possible meaning can it have today, when it is clearly so sorely lacking?

There are some paradoxes that I have to accept. I simply have no choice. That particular one is essential, and it is equally essential to face it, though I have found no way to resolve it. I do not understand it now, and I never will. I first asked this question more than forty years ago, and it is as valid today as ever. My only answer is that I would not like to see any one point of view prevail over the others. On the contrary, this must remain an open question, a conflict.

You would not argue that theodicy died in Auschwitz or that providence no longer exists?

I certainly do not agree with those who say: faith alone exists, faith stands above all else. That would amount to saying: have faith, and that's that. But neither would I agree with the claim that theodicy is dead. The moment an answer is given, I get suspicious; as a question, I accept it.

Isn't it true that every human being's life is dominated by the accident of having been born in one place and not in another?

On the contrary, in the Jewish tradition we believe that there is divine intervention, almost a divine choice. God foreordains each soul before its birth; each soul is His treasure, and He watches over it personally. There are no guardian angels. It is the Lord Himself who takes charge of His souls. In the midrashic legend, there is a sort of image depicting God giving life to a soul. It is He who wanted you to be born in one place and I in another. That is why I like to think that in this instance chance is not involved at all.

But consider the death of so many thousands of children, in places like Ethiopia and Somalia, Vietnam and Cambodia. Doesn't that attest to the absolute meaninglessness, the fundamental absurdity, of the human condition, after what you call the Event?

How can you reconcile this basic absurdity with the meaning of Jewish faith?

Yes, it is absurd, tragically absurd. It shows that our world has learned nothing. Perhaps there is nothing to learn; perhaps it is so far beyond our understanding that we cannot draw any conclusions. But we have to make the effort, and today even that is lacking. The fact that there is still so much suffering and so much agony, so many deaths and so many victims, shows that we—and all our contemporaries—have failed to bring man's deeds into line with his capacities.

Isn't this a terrible failure of human thought, and perhaps also of religion?

In this case the issue is not religion, but thought. The failure of religion came earlier, during the Whirlwind. It was then that we realized religion was no longer an effective pillar or source of strength or truth. For the most part, the killers had been baptized. They had been reared under Christianity, and some of them even went to church, to mass, and probably to confession. Yet still they killed. That showed that there was no barrier in Christianity preventing the killers from doing their evil.

What we are seeing today, on the other hand, is a failure of humanity, perhaps a failure of rationalism, but certainly a failure of politics and commitment, a failure of all systems, of philosophy, and of art.

Can this meaninglessness be reconciled with the meaning of religious faith?

My view is that faith must be tested. If it is unbroken, then it is not whole. "There is nothing so whole as a broken heart," Rabbi Nahman of Bratzlav once said. But in our epoch, I would say, there is nothing so whole as broken faith. Faith must be tested. But it must not remain severed or sundered. We must press on, facing up to what happened in the past and what is happening in the world today. We can no longer simply accept faith as such. We must first pass through a period of anguish, then one of respite, ultimately recovering and rediscovering the faith of our Masters. Because without faith we could not survive. Without faith our world would be empty.

In the terrifying twenty-sixth chapter of Vayikra (Leviticus), the word qeri *occurs seven times in succession. Most translations render it as "defiance," or "with harshness, stubbornness." But Rabbi Ben Ouziel in the Talmud, Maimonides in his epistle to Yemen, and André Neher (among others) have translated this word as* chance. *Neher, for instance, translates: "If you choose the covenant, I will be with you in the covenant. If you choose chance, I will yet be with you in chance." How do you interpret this duality, this counterposition between Obedience and Chance, between the choice of Covenant and the choice of Chance?*

I agree. In my view, this is the only meaning: qeri means chance. On another level, it also connotes chaos, which is the enemy of everything the Jewish religion holds dear. Chaos is worse than chance, worse than any-thing, because if there is chaos, then Good is not good and Evil is boundless. It is the original *tohu va bohu*. *Qeri* is therefore chance, and with chance anything is possi-ble. Covenant, on the contrary, is a response to chance. We have a choice between Covenant and Chance, and it is incumbent upon us to formulate that choice, to accept it, and to make it. Moreover, it is a choice that must be made daily. Each and every day we have the power, the privilege, of saying to ourselves: today either I partake of Covenant or I am here by chance.

Isn't this the first question we ask ourselves within faith itself?

Except that within faith we must sometimes take our stand against chance, but never against Covenant. In other words, I can protest against God within the Cove-nant, but not outside it.

Recently you said, "it is my faith, my confidence in God and His promises, that has been shaken." On the other hand, you have also said that although you are sometimes for God and of-ten against Him, you are never without Him.

That is exactly how I would describe my relationship to my faith. I have never foresaken it, and it has never foresaken me. Whatever has been shaken has been shaken within faith, for faith has always been present. The question was: what is happening in the world, why is it happening, according to what design? So yes, there is a shaking of faith, but there is also faith, and there is protest against faith precisely because it has been shaken.

Have you ever found it impossible to say certain prayers?

Not any more, but it used to happen to me often. To-day I know that heartbreak exists, and that prayer is tied to heartbreak. In the morning prayer, for instance, there is a phrase that says *Ashrenu ma-tov 'helkenu,* "happy are we with our destiny! How pleasant is our fate! How precious is our heritage!" When I think that I recited that prayer in the camp, along with hundreds of my comrades, that we said it again and again! How could we have said such a prayer? Yet we did. So I tell myself that if we said it in the camp, what right do I have to stop saying it today?

Yet there are dreadful—perhaps even dreadfully unutterable—prayers in the Rosh Hashanah [New Year] ritual, in which we say that on Yom Kippur [the Day of Atonement] the book of God records the fate of those who will live and those who will die in the course of the year, whether by illness or famine, war or fire, flood or epidemic. How can we recite such prayers?

Nevertheless, I accept them.

But shouldn't they be understood metaphorically and allegorically rather than literally?

life after death

Of course they should be understood metaphorically. Which simply means: I believe that there is some connection between what we do and what happens to us.

But what is the connection between these prayers and the thousands of starving people in Africa and elsewhere? Could they prevent famine by doing something different, by believing in something else?

It is our duty to see to it that these thousands of people suffer less, and that fewer of them—or none at all—die of famine. Which simply means that in one way or another, we are responsible for their fate.

In the darkest and most terrible moments of doubt and despair, what was your response to the summons in Devarim (Deuteronomy): "Choose life that you may live"? In particular, what meaning do you attach to the second clause of the verse: that you may live? Why the repetition? Could one choose life that one might not live?

Quran

One could choose life so as not to live and one could live life so as to proclaim the end of life. Nietzscheans and the philosophers of the absurd speak of life against life. What the Torah is saying is that one must choose life in order to live and to sanctify life. In my view, we must first of all say, "choose life." And second: "choose the living." A single living being is more important than all the dead who have gone before.

In this sense, your memory and your work are for the living?

I write for the living, but I would also like to reconcile them to the dead, for in our century a terrible breach has opened between the living and the dead. It may be that the two are also divided by a terrible rage, and that's why I think it is high time to try to reconcile them.

Is there any such thing as survivor's guilt? Is there a special responsibility or difficulty of being a Jew after the Shoah?

all

A special difficulty, no. If anything, it's easier. Things are much clearer today. We have seen that assimilation is no solution, that weakness is no solution, that abdication is no solution. So at least we know that the only solution for a Jew is to live within his Jewishness. That makes it easier. Each of us can say yes or no, but either way, at least we know. In the eighteenth century, during the Emancipation and the Enlightenment, there was conflict within the community: how far should we go in emancipating ourselves? Today we know that it is all very well to live in a particular society, that it is important to adapt to it; but a Jew can do this only within his Jewishness. On that there is no choice. Either one is a Jew or one is not. We can reject the Covenant or accept it, but if we accept it, then we must position and define ourselves within it.

Don't Jews today have a greater responsibility toward the Jews who perished in the Whirlwind? Emil Fackenheim speaks of a 614th mitzvah [in Jewish Law there are 613 mitzvoth, or divine commandments], which he calls "the prescriptive voice of Auschwitz."

We have an obligation to the dead. Their memory must be kept alive. I like Fackenheim very much. He is a friend of mine, and I esteem his attitude, his thought, and his work. He is a great Jewish philosopher who has unfortunately not been accorded the recognition he deserves. He is right to say that we have a special responsibility to the dead. Indeed, to have survived only in order to forget would be blasphemy, a second catastrophe. To forget the dead would be to have them die a second time.

Do you feel a special calling? Hasn't the Nobel Peace Prize affirmed and confirmed the mission with which you have been identified — the duty of memory, of zakhor — and the testimony you have embodied for nearly thirty years now?

I am not looking for confirmation of anything. The judgment others may make of me is not important to me and never has been. I do not feel that any particular duty suddenly descended upon me simply because of the Nobel Prize. Like all Jews who survived the war, I am

conscious of a duty, one that everyone assumes in his
own way. Mine has been to study, to exalt study, and
most of all to try not to leave the world to its good conscience. That is why I have often glorified victims and
survivors, though I am well aware that not all of them
were by any means saints. Some of them may simply not
have been up to it, but that is beside the point. I leave
it to others to speak ill of them. For my part, I prefer to
speak well. Then perhaps the world might realize how
much it lost when it allowed six million Jews to be killed.
How many Nobel Prize winners might there have been
among the million and a half children who were killed?
Perhaps some of those dead Nobel Prize winners—
murdered at the age of two, six, or eight—might have
discovered a cure for cancer or for AIDS. The world must
understand the punishment it suffered by allowing
these crimes to be committed. Many of those million and
a half dead children, for example, might have traveled,
immigrated to the United States or Israel. The majority
of American Nobel Prize winners were born in central
Europe.

*Your work is laden with compassion, with rejection of death
and hatred, with forgiveness and a fundamental aversion to
vengeance. Are these qualities the deepest personal victory you
have snatched from the hell you suffered?*

"Victory" is too strong a word. How can we speak of
victory in a world in which the dead remain dead? If they
could be brought back to life, that would be a victory; but
since they cannot be brought back, the word is mis-
placed. Nor is the word "forgive" appropriate. I am not
concerned with forgiveness. Conciliation yes, but not
forgiveness. Perhaps I can forgive what they did to me,
but nobody appointed me to speak for others. Last year
I went to Germany for a conference. I reminded my audience that Germany, after all, had occupied Poland and

the Ukraine, France and Greece, and other countries as well. But only the Jewish people are constantly asked, "Why don't you forgive?" Why don't they ask forgiveness of France, Holland, Belgium, Poland, the Soviet Union? But the truth is, they haven't even asked the Jews for forgiveness. Germany has never asked the Jewish people to forgive. And suppose the Bundestag did pass a resolution saying, Let us officially ask forgiveness of the Jews. Then it would be up to Jerusalem, to the State of Israel, to respond. By what right could a writer like me answer?

Chancellor Willy Brandt knelt before the monument to the ghetto in Warsaw. That, after all, was an important gesture.

It was a gesture of mourning. He did not ask forgiveness.

Responsibility and Meaning

Philippe de Saint-Cheron: *Can the ethic that runs through our entire Bible be seen as a response to a world in which the most basic human rights can be (and are) trampled underfoot, a response to a civilization whose morality teaches that anything that is possible is permissible, and in which, it would seem, we have no rights but only duties?*

Elie Wiesel: It is the only response. There is no other. There is so much violence in this world, so much terror and inhumanity, that we must try to return to an ancient wisdom. What are ethics, at bottom? They are laws that govern the relations between human beings. They govern the relationship between me and others, not between me and God. So long as these ethics are not explored, shared, and adopted, we are in danger.

The whole power and grandeur of Jewish thought—which is not incarnated in any supreme authority and is in essence antidogmatic—lies in the assertion that man's transcendence to God occurs through his neighbors: through widows, orphans, foreigners, the poor. Wouldn't you agree?

The Torah teaches us: *Veahavta lereakha kamokha, ani Adoshem,* "You shall love your neighbor as yourself. I am the Lord." What is the connection? There is none. "You shall love your neighbor as yourself. I am the Lord." Which means, precisely, that the Lord is tied to love. My divinity is expressed through your humanity. Elsewhere (and at another level), God tells the Jewish people: *Edim atem ladoshem,* "You are my witnesses." The Talmud comments: If you are my witnesses, then I am God, and if you are not my witnesses, then I am not God. Here again, it is our witness that determines God's divinity and eternity.

Do you think that man's wisdom has evolved as quickly as science and technology, or is the gap between them wider than ever?

The gap can be measured in light-years. This is one of the reasons why we often feel such despair. In medicine, the sciences, nuclear physics, computer technology, the human race has made more progress in the past fifty years than in the previous three thousand. But in philosophy, literature, poetry, religion, and morality, there has been very little progress at all. True, from time to time we see an advance here and there; but it is slow, maddeningly slow.

Why is it that religions are so insistent on absolving God from guilt? Is a silent God any more acceptable than an indifferent, deaf, or insane God? In Twilight, *one of your characters, Boris, declares: "I am God because I am guilty, guiltier than all human beings put together."*

Don't forget that this is a madman talking. On the other hand, the issue has to be faced. Deep down, I feel certain — and this is a Jewish certitude drawn from the sources of tradition — that an indifferent God is incomprehensible and inconceivable. An unjust God, yes. Indeed, who am I to judge God's justice, or His attitude to justice? But an indifferent God is impossible. God's creation of man itself speaks against indifference. One does not create out of indifference. On the contrary, Creation is a protest against indifference. The fact that God participates in history and in destiny bears witness that He is man's friend and is not alien to him.

"We are all guilty of everything, and I am the most guilty of all," Dostoyevsky wrote in The Brothers Karamazov. *In the Sota treatise of the Babylonian Talmud it is written that everyone is responsible for everyone else. Isn't the guilt of which Dostoyevsky speaks simply the negative side of responsibility, and isn't there a danger that this kind of responsibility is so impossible that it can lead to indifference?*

That depends. If you try to start everywhere all at once, you get nowhere, but if you start with very small, personal things, then the circle of responsibility can be widened. When we try to help everyone at once, we usually wind up helping no one at all. But if I start with a single person—someone near to me, a friend or a neighbor—then I can in turn come nearer to others.

During the war the entire world knew of the existence of Auschwitz, yet the railroads leading there were never bombed. Isn't this irrefutable accusation still valid today? What did the West, or the world, do during the Vietnam War, or the war in Cambodia, which continues even now, or in Bangladesh, or in the Iran-Iraq war? What is being done to save the Boat People or those dying of hunger?

 Past indifference has engendered today's indifference. If the world let things go between 1939 and 1945, why not let things go today? This is a dreadful but logical chain of reasoning. It is punishment. The world is punishing itself. Unfortunately, the children are paying the price, and that is unjust. Our duty is to sound the alarm, to shout, to protest, even to weep in the public square.

You have said that because ghettos existed during the war, they can no longer exist. Yet in a sense they do, even right here in New York City. Harlem gives every sign of being a ghetto for blacks. And what about South Africa?

In the context of Jewish history, the holocaust against the Jewish people can no longer recur, but it is true that other peoples, other communities, have been or are being struck by other tragedies: Cambodia, Bangladesh, Ireland, Lebanon (which is in the process of commiting suicide), Ethiopia. And then there are the ghettos of South Africa. I insisted on going to Soweto, Pretoria's great ghetto, to tell the black community how deeply concerned I was by its fate and by the fate of Nelson Mandela.

Aren't the Palestinian camps somehow comparable to ghettos?

No, I cannot make that comparison. As a Jew who experienced Nazism, I cannot possibly make that kind of analogy. Unlike leftists and revolutionaries, I do not consider the Palestinians today's "Jews." So far as I know, they are not threatened with extermination as we, the Jews, were during the war.

But isn't the fate of the thousands of Palestinians living in the camps, especially the women and children, terrible and unjust?

I am moved and concerned by their tragedy, especially that of the children, the young people. I know that something must be done, which is why I referred to their misfortune in my Oslo speech. I said this: "I am sensitive to their suffering, but I deplore their methods when they lead to violence." And I added: "The Jewish people and the Palestinian people have lost too many children and

have shed too much blood since 1948: it is time to stop."
But as a Jew, I think it is only natural that my loyalty and
love go first to Israel, just as it is natural for a Palestinian's love and loyalty to go first to his people.

*In Europe, as well as in the United States, tons of food—
enough to feed millions of hungry people—lie rotting in enormous warehouses. The philosopher Jürgen Habermas, among
others, has asked this question: "Is the conquest of space really
more urgent than the satisfaction of the basic needs of entire
continents whose people are suffering from famine?" Is our
Western civilization condemned to let millions of victims of fate
die?*

I would like to be able to say no. Powerful countries
are trying to conquer space. But nothing is being done
to bring us closer to our neighbors. I know more about
the moon than I do about what lies in my neighbor's
heart. If only I knew his heart—to use a Hasidic
paraphrase—I would know his needs and might be able
to do something to help. But the fact is that famine,
tragedy, and human despair are no longer front-page
news in our epoch. The Boat People are still drowning
in the sea or being slaughtered, the women raped by
pirates. Day after day, their tragedy goes on. For how
long? Yet how many newspapers still cover that tragedy? In Cambodia, people cross the border into Thailand
every day. All this suffering, all this misery, continues.
But few people show any interest, and fewer still are
moved.

*Three of your books are devoted to the Jews of silence. Do you
believe that the faith and loyalty of the Jews of the Soviet Union
give meaning to our freedom, or do you feel that part of the
meaning of that freedom is to lend our voice to these men and
women who live their faith with such daily heroism? Is it not*

a moral obligation, a religious duty, for us to remain faithful
to our tradition, to our faith?

I am so fully a part of their struggle! I consider their
heroism one of the most beautiful chapters of our life;
and their faith is one of the most beautiful signs of courage and devotion in our vocabulary. So long as they are
not free, we are not free either. So long as they cannot
live their lives as Jews, our Jewish life is not complete.
It borders on the criminal to say that our concerns are not
theirs or theirs not ours. We are deeply and wholly involved in this. If they are imprisoned, it is partly our
fault, and if some have been released, it is partly thanks
to us. If others still languish, it is surely because we have
not done enough to bring about their freedom.

In Paroles d'étranger *you wrote: "in my small hometown*
in the Carpathians, I knew the reason for my existence: to
glorify God and to sanctify His word. . . . I knew that I be-
longed to His chosen people—the people chosen to serve Him
through suffering and hope. I knew that I lived in an exile that
was complete, universal, and even cosmic."
Do you really believe that the Jewish people cannot live free
of ordeals and suffering?

We have not yet had the chance to live free of ordeals.
But I still believe that we could and that we should.
Suffering is not something we need. The greatest Jewish
works of poetry, philosophy, astronomy, biblical commentary, and exegesis were produced during the Gold-
en Age in Spain. If we are allowed some respite, we
would contribute a bit of light, a bit of warmth and grace,
for the good of the world and the glory of humanity.

Asceticism and love of suffering do not seem to be genuine
Jewish values. Is asceticism something you have been much
concerned with?

I have been quite concerned with it, both before and after the war. This is still an open question. Does suffering have any meaning? And if an individual's suffering has meaning, would that imply that the suffering of a people, a community, has an even higher meaning? Would it then follow that one kind of suffering is somehow more lofty than the others, that it has a higher, more worthy, or more honorable significance? This is a question that has always intrigued me.

And do you have an answer?

The answer lies in the Jewish tradition, which denies the value of suffering. We do not believe that suffering can create or engender anything that transcends it. Suffering is not something one chooses. It is a persistent mystery, and we therefore try to make something of it. But, I repeat, it would be against tradition to choose suffering.

But didn't Rabbi Akiba speak of suffering for love?

It is true that there is a difference between two kinds of suffering: *ahavat yissurin* and *yissurin shel ahava*. *Yissurin shel ahava* denotes the suffering that comes from love. That we accept. But *ahavat yissurin*, love of suffering, is something else. That we do not accept. In those days, suffering had meaning for the Jews, most probably because there was no alternative but to suffer. But had it been possible not to suffer, the Jews would surely not have chosen suffering simply out of love for it.

Yet suffering is an ubiquitous question in Hasidism.

Hasidism was a protest against suffering. Earlier there had been a period of cabalistic asceticism during which some thought that truth could be attained through suffering. But later the Baal Shem Tov, Master of the

Good Name, proclaimed that truth could not be attained through suffering. Another way was proposed. God could be attained not through suffering or distress, but through song and joy. Subsequently, of course, Hasidism did deal with suffering, but always to denounce it.

How have Jewish tradition and Hasidism interpreted Evil and death? In Isaiah we read: "I form the light and create darkness: I make peace and create evil: I, the Lord, do all these things."

And in the first book of Samuel, Hannah proclaims: "The Lord puts to death and gives life." Is Adam and Eve's offense the cause of the death and evil that has dwelled within man?

This is primarily a philosophical idea advanced in opposition to the notion of divine duality: a god of good and a god of evil. Isaiah was proclaiming the oneness of God. God is one; He is everywhere. And if He is everywhere, then He is in evil and injustice too, and also in the supreme evil: death. It is man's task to free God of this evil. Every time we extirpate a spark of evil, we hasten the coming of the Messiah.

André Malraux, though an agnostic, wrote: "No one can avoid death, but man alone can give his life." And in Man's Fate: *"what value has a life that has not accepted death?"*

Isn't it true that death can sometimes acquire a meaning that in turn attests to the meaning of life? And can't this be seen as an attempt to overcome Evil and absurdity?

Malraux was a writer for whom artistic form was as important as content. What he is saying here is convincing because he relates it to the Chinese revolution.

But the Jewish tradition is completely different, because suicide is forbidden. For us there are only three prohibitions so severe that it is our duty to choose death over transgression. These are murder, adultery, and idolatry. If an enemy was in a position to force us to commit one of these three crimes, then we would have to die instead. [See Maimonides, *The Book of Knowledge*, chapter 5.] In other words, I must sacrifice my own life rather than take another's, and I must choose death rather than commit adultery, which dishonors an entire family, bringing shame upon them. The final prohibition concerns idolatry: I must not bow down before an idol, lest I lose all self-respect not only before God but also before my own people, and thus before humanity. A man who bows down to an idol made by other men repudiates himself.

When we look at the fighting between—and even within—religions, should we not wonder whether historically they have been sources of conflict, disaster, and war, rather than founts of peace and fraternal love?

Up to now, that is indeed the impression they give, what with all the wars, violence, fear, and intolerance. This is not salvation but its opposite. The truth is that it is up to us to change.

In Vie et destin *Vasily Grossman writes: "Men who yearn for the good of humanity are powerless to reduce the evil on this earth."*
But isn't the opposite equally true: that men who do evil are powerless to reduce or annihilate human goodness and kindness?

Sometimes, yes.

Do you believe that evil is stronger than good?

Unfortunately, those who commit evil are stronger. One killer with a machine gun triumphs over a thousand sages. It's as simple as that. The killer is armed, and his victims are not.

The television coverage of the Armero disaster in Colombia in 1985 included shots of a little girl vainly crying to her mother for help. Do you think pictures like that should be shown on television?

I don't know. It is important to move people, but also to avoid trivializing tragedy. I am very much afraid of trivialization. If people see too many such images, they become deaf and dumb, indifferent and apathetic. They are tempted to let themselves be permanent spectators. The tenth time they see the image, they no longer react as they did the first time. They may not even react at all.

But isn't there also a danger that these unbearable images might arouse morbid instincts?

No. A movement of broad solidarity cannot be morbid. On the contrary, it is a means of conquering morbidity. There is nothing more beautiful than the sight of a human community joining together to rescue a little girl.

But don't you see a difference between human solidarity on the one hand and the photo or footage shot by the reporter on the other?

Personally, I don't. In fact, I would be quite literally incapable of separating the two. Don't forget that the movement of solidarity arose exactly because a journalist filmed the scene.

The Sota treatise of the Talmud [12a] states that to attain olam haba, *the world above, one must first be born in* olam hazeh, *this world. Do you believe that the mystery of* having been *(of which Vladimir Yankelovich speaks in his book* La Mort) *is sufficient proof that all is not vanity, that all is not lost?*

I have no need of *olam haba* to know or to believe that all is not vanity in our world. It is not *olam haba* that determines the world above. As I see it, all is not in vain even if that little girl could not be saved. Other images have saved other little girls, and they will do so again in the future. No, all is not futile.

The conclusion of your latest novel, Twilight, *shows quite profoundly that it is impossible to offer facile consolation, to promise that ultimately everything will work out. Your character Raphael remains faithful to his dead friend to the very end despite everything—even despite God Himself. Doesn't this show that Judaism is an adult religion?*

But it is also a child's religion. You know how important children are in our tradition.

What I mean is that it is a faith that offers no instant promises or consolation.

It is true that Judaism is a lucid religion not made up of other-worldly dreams.

Emmanuel Levinas showed me a passage in the treatise Hagigah that speaks to this point very directly: "Rabbi Ami wept when he read these lines in *Lamentations*: 'He put his mouth to the dust: there may yet be hope.' And he added: 'So much evil and only perhaps is there hope!' "

But you know very well that you can also find the contrary in the treatise Hagigah.

Even so, the passage seems emblematic both of the Jewish worldview and of the modernity of the incomparable Masters of the talmudic epoch.

Yes. One of the remarkable things about our tradition, our faith, is precisely that both positions—options as contradictory as hope and despair, with an abyss between them—can be accepted within Judaism. You know Rabba's famous saying: "I yearn, I hope, for the coming of the Messiah, but I would not like to see him." In other words: I want him to come, but I do not want to be there to greet him.

A fearsome and incomprehensible statement!

Fearsome, yes, but you can also find other *hakhamim* [sages of the talmudic epoch] who say: I would give my life to be present on that day.

For a century, the contributions made by Jews to humanity were not at all religious and were often even hostile to Judaism. The nineteenth century saw the rise and development of true intellectual and social revolutions, with Marx and Freud in particular. In the twentieth century, however—especially since the war—specifically Jewish, and therefore spiritually universal, values have been proclaimed by such men as Buber, Scholem, Cassin, Agnon, and Singer (the latter two Nobel Laureates in Literature), as well as Levinas and yourself, among others. Does this mark a revival of Jewish spirituality?

It's true that there is fresh interest, but I am not at all sure that I would call it a revival. Don't forget that a very powerful Jewish spirituality came into the world in the eighteenth century with the birth of the Hasidic movement and the flowering and glory of the Gaon of Vilna. But truly great men are few indeed today. Perhaps what intrigues the world is the survival of Jewish spirituality despite all the evils and all the threats. Israel's endurance through history intrigues the world. How did you manage to survive? How have you managed to remain what you are? How is it that you have not foundered, not given way, not despaired? That is what interests the world. And it is true that we seem to possess a kind of key, the key to survival.

Do you feel that humanity is awaiting an answer that only the Jews can provide?

The world is certainly calling upon us, asking questions of us. It is no longer we who are asking questions of the world (for historically we have always asked questions of the peoples around us), but the world that is questioning us. How did you do it? Teach us the art of survival! And it is true that of all the peoples of antiquity, we alone have survived. This poses a problem, but at the same time it gives us both a duty and a privilege.

Don't you think that alongside this privilege there is also a paradigm, in the sense that what Levinas calls the Passion of Israel has a universal significance? Let me cite a particularly revealing example. When the pope went to South Korea, the leading Korean daily newspaper ran an editorial that said, among other things, "As the Sovereign Pontiff knows, the Korean people have suffered from the logic of an immoral force during the past two centuries, just like the Israelites."
Doesn't this reference to Jewish suffering, on the other side of the world, attest to its universal significance?

Absolutely. We serve as a point of reference, a paradigm.

In a certain sense, hasn't hatred of the Jews been displaced? Today all ethnic and racial minorities are threatened with suffering or already subjected to it: the blacks in South Africa,

the Turks in Germany, the poor within the rich countries,
sometimes called the fourth world.

Yes, but all this has not lessened hatred of the Jews.
You say that this hatred has been displaced, yet it persists. In fact, I would say that it has spread. People who
hate the Jews also hate the other minorities. It's not like
a bank where you take money out of one account and de-
posit it in another. There is enough hatred to hate the entire world: the Jews, the Turks, the Armenians, the
blacks, the Hispanic Americans, and especially in
France, the Arabs. There are many victims of hatred,
which always comes from the same source. Those who
hate one group inevitably hate the others. Those who
hate the Jews hate all minorities.

In several of your books you refer to another kind of suffer-
ing, which you experienced in your own life in France just after
the war: material poverty and hunger. How do you react to the
rising poverty in the industrialized countries? The obvious
poverty in the streets of New York, for example, is especially
alarming.

Yes, it is. It's horrible. The food thrown away by New
York restaurants could feed the continent of Africa. We
protest, we raise our voices, we sound the alarm to
governments. What else can we do? Unfortunately, I am
convinced that the industrial countries are going to pay
dearly for this crime, and I use the term advisedly. We
know that there are people dying of hunger and disease,
and it would cost so little to send them food, medicine,
doctors, nurses. We are going to pay dearly for this.

When we speak of Israel as the chosen people, we are refer-
ring, essentially, to the ineluctable responsibility that we were
just discussing, and not, as far too many people think, to any
special privileges. Would you agree?

The truth is that it is neither the one nor the other. The selection of Israel is an example. We say that Israel is a chosen, or selected, people, but we also say that any people has the right to say the same about itself.

Every people is therefore a chosen people?

Every people can be chosen and can see itself as chosen, just as we call ourselves chosen. But chosen by virtue of what: what suffering, what plan? Every people has the same right as we do to conceive of itself as different but not superior.

The Shma Israel, the most famous Jewish prayer, one we recite twice daily, contains this verse: Ani Adoshem Elohek hem asher hotzeti etekhem meeretz Mitzraim, *"I am the Lord your God, which brought you out of the land of Egypt." Can we say that the Jew who pronounces these words in the stead of and* for *the Lord thereby partakes of His Essence, thus participating in the liberation of all the wretched of the earth?*

I cannot say that I partake of God. God is in me, as He is in every being, and every human being is born of His Being. But it is a little arrogant to say, It is I who helped God bring us out of Egypt.

But given the situation in the world today, don't we have the right to ask whether a Jew who helps free the Jews of the Soviet Union (or any other human beings deprived of liberty) in some sense partakes of this selection?

I don't think we ought to go so far. It must be done because it must be done. Because God has done it. Because in ancient times, when we were aliens in the land of Egypt, we felt a solidarity, or we ought to have felt it, with all aliens, all victims. We must help others not because we are God, but because we are human. The verse must be read in its proper context, on the basis of the entire Jewish tradition.

Do you believe that the masses of the poor countries will someday revolt and attack the rich countries? I am thinking of the masses of South America in particular.

It's possible, except that the problem in South America is different. True, many men, women, and children there are suffering from hunger, poverty, and disease, but this is an entire continent, and concrete possibilities of helping these people exist. So does the will to do so.

On the other hand, it is undeniable that we are seeing a rise of violence in all the world's cities. The punishment has already begun.

You recently returned from Japan. Was it the first time you had been there? What was the purpose of your trip?

Yes, it was my first visit. I went to attend several conferences and also to to bear witness, to demonstrate my interest and compassion. Which is only natural. As I see it, Auschwitz was an end, but Hiroshima was a beginning.

You mean that Hiroshima was possible because Auschwitz had occurred?

Yes. I have said so, and that is what I believe. Once again, if the world was capable of allowing the massacre of millions of children, women, and old people, why not also allow the annihilation of a city? But the thought that Hiroshima was a beginning is truly terrifying. And I feel very strongly that it was. There will be no more Auschwitzes; that's over with. But there may well be more Hiroshimas.

Evil and Love

Philippe de Saint-Cheron: *It seems to me that raising the question of Evil inevitably raises the question of Good, of love. What are your feelings about the people who were able to demonstrate the greatest love, giving of themselves completely, even in the hell of the camps? I have in mind in particular the Polish Franciscan Maximilian Kolbe, whose church declared him the saint and martyr of the camps.*

Elie Wiesel: Personally, I think more about the people I knew, about the Jews—rabbis and laymen alike—who shared tenderness and generosity even in the camps. And indeed, I knew such people. They weren't saints, simply men and women who accepted their fate in very human and very Jewish terms. In fact, for them that meant the same thing, as it does for me as well. There are no saints in Judaism, of course; we do not believe in them. Sainthood is divine. In the Shma Israel we say: *vihitem kedoshim lelohekhem*, may you be holy unto your God. In other words, may you be sanctified. In place of saints we have the Just; it is they who serve as examples.

In One Generation After *you talk about a man you met in Auschwitz whom you call the prophet.*

Yes, he was a visionary. I have known some exceptional people in my life. Even there.

*People can sometimes become exceptional in particularly in-
human and tragic circumstances, don't you think?*

Yes, I do.

*If I'm not mistaken, you have never discussed the sublime
figure of Janusz Korczak, the Polish Jewish educator whose
work has been translated into several languages in the past few
years and to whom the International Year of the Child was
dedicated in 1978. He was the founder of the House of Orphans
in Warsaw. On August 4, 1942, he rejected the clemency the
Nazis had offered him and voluntarily agreed to accompany the
two hundred Jewish children of his ghetto orphanage to Treblinka, where he died in the gas chamber.*

The reason I rarely speak of Korczak is that I did not
know him personally. As you say, he was in the Warsaw
ghetto, and I was living in Sighet.

Don't you find him a sublime figure?

Korczak was a very great man. He came from an assimilated family, and it was only in the ghetto that he
really proved what he was made of. He chose to live and
die with the children rather than survive without them.
Extraordinary. Although he was not religious, I think of
him as a kind of lay rabbi. I have a deep admiration for
him.
But so many rabbis followed their disciples to their
deaths. In almost every city of central Europe, the rabbis
had a chance to save themselves by taking refuge in
churches or monasteries, yet 99 percent of them—
thousands in all—refused, because they felt that their
place was with the community, with their disciples and
their families. Just like Korczak. Or perhaps it was Korczak who was just like them.

Curiously, it is not in Judaism's nature to bestow any partic-
ular adoration upon such people: the Just, genuine martyrs of
love. Unlike the Church.

Yes, this is one of the differences between us and the
Church, between Jews and Catholics.

You are familiar with the moving Journal *of Etty Hillesum,*
the Dutch Jewish woman who died in Auschwitz at about the
age of twenty-four. In her diary she explains how she came to
see love even during the Nazi occupation. She wrote that terri-
ble phrase: "If all this suffering does not bring about . . . a
greater humanity, . . . then it will have been in vain."

I think that there was indeed a burst of humanity, but
it came from the survivors themselves and not from the
world that watched them emerge from the hell.

Then it was not all in vain, if it is permissible to say such
a thing.

That must remain an open question. If we said that
the suffering was not in vain, that might sound as
though we were justifying it. The life and death of a single child is more important than all the answers, all the
tenderness, all the humanity in the world. But at the
same time, it would be just as awful to say that the
suffering had been in vain, for that would be to indict not
only the living, but also the dead, whose suffering and
death would then be seen as having been unable to engender the burst of humanity that we are talking about.
That is why I believe that both answers must remain
open.

You often recount a curious story from the Pessahim treatise
of the Talmud. There are two men in the desert, one of whom
has a gourd of water, but not enough to save them both. Ben

Petura states unhesitatingly: "let them share it, even if they both must die!" But Rabbi Akiba objects, "No, for it is said khayekha kodmin: *your life stands higher, it does not belong to you. Let the owner of the gourd drink his water." Isn't that a terrible thing to say: that you do not have the right to forfeit your own life for another's sake, since your life does not belong to you?*

What meaning would you ascribe to Rabbi Akiba's statement today?

In general, the law cited by Rabbi Akiba is directed against suicide. That is its primary meaning. We do not have the right to commit suicide, because life—including our own life—does not belong to us. It was given to us by God, and only its proprietor, God Himself, has the right to dispose of it. Today, I would argue, the saying has a different meaning: that we are responsible not only for our own lives but also for the lives of those who might live in our stead. It is as if Rabbi Akiba had said, for example: the man must share his water with his friend, for the friend might live in place of the survivor. What I mean is that the survivor can live on in the place of—and in some sense for—the one who dies. That is the privilege and curse of all survival: it entails a debt to the dead.

This, no doubt, is the responsibility that Jews must shoulder in our epoch: to try to be Jewish for the sake of those who died in the Whirlwind.

Perhaps every Jew ought to pick a dead man, woman, or child, whether known or unknown, and say: from this point on, I shall live for myself and for him or her. Then perhaps all of us together, both for ourselves and for them, might someday rebuild the life and destiny, faith and fear, and most of all the song—the eternal song—of an eternal people.

On December 25, 1939, Chaim A. Kaplan wrote in his
Chronicle of Agony, *a Journal of the Warsaw Ghetto: "It
is a 'holiday' today, and all the nations of the world are celebrat-
ing the birth of their savior. Their savior, not ours. And there
lies the cause of the whole Jewish tragedy. If we, too, were to
say 'Our Savior,' then the hatred against us would not be so
great." Have you ever shared that view?*

No, because even if the Jewish people – and this is unthinkable, inconceivable – had adopted the Christian
faith, I don't think it would have lessened the hatred
against us. This hatred is metaphysical. The Talmud itself considers this question, and asks: "Why is the
mountain on which the Torah was given to our Master
Moses called Sinai? Because that is where the word *sinah*
[hatred] comes from." Hatred of the Jews was born with
the Torah, and the Torah predates Christianity. There
was anti-Semitism among the Romans, who were pa-
gans. They were not Christians, yet they hated the Jews.
It cannot be said, therefore, that Christianity alone
spawned the hatred of the Jews that we see throughout
history. There would have been anti-Semitism even
without Christianity, although Christianity certainly
contributed to broadening it and to spreading it
throughout the world.

Why is it that you hardly ever use the word shoah *but often
say "Holocaust"? Isn't that a blasphemous word?*

Yes, but all words are blasphemous, including *shoah*.
No word is adequate to describe this Event. *Shoah* was
chosen by Ben Gurion.

*But isn't the word "holocaust" – with its suggestion of
expiation – even worse?*

No, because *shoah* denotes a natural cataclysm, and this was not a natural cataclysm; it was perpetrated by men. An earthquake on a continental scale might be called *shoah*, but that is not what we are talking about here. This was not a rebellion of nature; men were responsible for it.

But shoah *was the word used by the prophet Sophonias to designate catastrophe, wasn't it?*

The biblical word denotes precisely a natural catastrophe. It is not the right word. It was accepted in France because Israel accepted it, but from the outset I chose "holocaust," which emphasizes the mystical, religious texture of the tragedy, indicating that it was not simply one more pogrom like the many that had gone before, nor was it a mere consequence of war. This Catastrophe was redolent of fire above all else. In that sense I find it a more powerful word than *shoah*. What does "holocaust" mean? Total offering by fire. Now, if we have to use some word, "fire" is probably the clearest. Fire was the dominant image in this tragedy. The term also implies total consumption, total sacrifice. Personally, the reason I don't like the word "holocaust" anymore is that it has been so trivialized and commercialized. These days it's used to refer to just about anything.

But it is also a word that some Christians, Claudel for example, have used blasphemously, identifying it with the famous Christian prediction of "the mass conversion of the Jews in the final days." Levinas has written that for Claudel, "the holocaust of millions of victims under Hitler" was representative of this conversion. And he added, referring to this particular view of the Jewish people: "For once, Holy History's incorrigible latecomer was on time." That's what I meant when I said that the word is vile.

I didn't realize that Claudel had attributed this horrible significance to it. But even in the sense in which I mean it, "holocaust" is a terrible word, because it has been so trivialized that any little tragedy is called a holocaust nowadays. So I don't use the word anymore. In fact, I haven't for years.

For you Evil, or hatred, is still the great question, is it not?

Hatred is Evil and Evil dwells in hatred. The two go hand in hand. They partake of the same phenomenon, the same source. But that is not the problem. The problem is that evil is sometimes done not in its own name but in the name of love. How many massacres have been planned and committed in the name of love! Which brings us back to what we were discussing earlier today: chance and chaos. Think of the *havdala* service that we celebrate at the close of the sabbath. It marks the border between the holy and the profane—or to put it another way, between good and evil—separating the sabbath from the rest of the week. The first thing God did in the Creation was to divide the higher from the lower waters. Let good be good and evil be evil; then we know that we must serve one and combat the other. So it is very serious when evil takes on the appearance of good.

Do you think that the kashrut *[the Jewish dietary laws] can be interpreted as more than a set of practical rules: as a philosophical idea intended to help us to distinguish the pure from the impure? Or is that going too far?*

It's going too far. For everyone except the practicing Jew, you know, the *kashrut* is far more complex than those categories might suggest. As for me, I observe the *kashrut* without bothering about problems of that kind. Many emancipated people say that the *kashrut* makes sense from a health point of view. But that is not the reason I don't eat pork, for example. I don't eat it because the Bible forbids it.

But is it inconceivable that the Lord gave the Hebrews these orders precisely to teach them to distinguish the pure from the impure?

In the Torah there are *hukim* and *mishpatim*, laws and prescriptions. Some are comprehensible, while others are not, yet we must observe those too.

Why does Judaism see the impure as stronger than the pure? Is that a teaching of tradition?

No, it is not tradition, but life itself that teaches us that. In tradition, on the contrary, it is hoped that good will be stronger than evil, that the pure will be stronger than the impure. But in life it is the impure that wins out. There is always more impurity than purity, just as the impious are more numerous than the just, and the villains more numerous than saints.

But isn't the power that has been granted impurity over purity a terrible thing?

That power was granted simply to encourage us to separate them, to turn away from impurity.

What can we do to make the pure stronger than the impure?

We can shun the impure. What is the *kashrut*? It is the separation of the impure from the pure, the chaff from the kosher. It warns us against evil, for evil is alluring. Tradition says: Do not come near evil! *Tref* is alluring: do not come near it!

*And we thereby become stronger than evil, stronger than
the impure?*

We gain another power: we learn to distinguish what
is pure from what is not.

*I would like to return to the question of love, as it figures in
chapter 19, verse 18 of Vayikra [Leviticus]:* Veahavta lereakha kamokha, *you shall love your neighbor as yourself.*
*I know of two readings of this verse: Buber and Rosenzweig's
German translation of the Hebrew Bible gives "Love your
neighbor, he is like you." Levinas goes even further, separating
the word* kamokha *from the rest of the verse: "Love your
neighbor: this love is yourself."*
What is your interpretation of this verse?

Levinas's is not a typical interpretation. I don't think
it is a *pshat*, or simple interpretation, but rather a *drash*,
or elicited meaning. (Which, by the way, confirms the
originality of Levinas's thought.) But I don't think this is
the current interpretation as it has been handed down
from generation to generation. To begin with, let's go
back to the text itself, to the *pshat*: love your neighbor,
love another, as yourself. Disturbing questions definitely arise here, and the Talmud deals with them. For instance, suppose you despise yourself; does that mean
that you should also despise your neighbor?
The literal translation is therefore "love your neighbor
as yourself." If you love him as yourself, that's fine. If
you value his interests as highly as your own, that's not
bad either. But we must also consider the conclusion of
the verse, which is often forgotten: *ani Hashem*, I am
God. What does this mean? It is I [God] who judge what
is good for you and for others; it is not for you to judge.
And what does this mean? Simply that you must grant
your friend the right to judge too. In other words, it is
not for you to tell your friend: I am better than you, I

know better than you do what's good for you. God alone knows what is good for both of you, because God stands above us, and only He knows the ultimate Good.

Doesn't the fact that this is a commandment suggest that man was not capable of loving his neighbor on his own?

Certainly. But the essential thing is that God knows what is good for me and what is good for you. I do not have the right to decide. That is the point of the caesura, the rift, in the phrase itself. You shall love your neighbor as yourself *because* I am God. You do not know what is good for your neighbor, but I, the Lord, know everything. I thought that Levinas was trying to say something else, that he would split the phrase differently, saying *veahavta lereakha, kamokha ani adoshem*: you shall love your neighbor, for, like you, I am God. In other words: I, too, am like that; I, God, love you as you love me. That strikes me as an even bolder reading. Perhaps Levinas did not dare to go all the way.

But you just did!
Nevertheless, this is a century of immense crowds, and I wonder whether crowds are not intrinsically prone to annihilate the spirit of love in the heart of the individual. Individuals feel crushed, lost in a human sea, as though losing their souls.

Think of all the millions of people watching television at the same time. They are alone, yet they are also part of an enormous crowd viewing the same images at the same time. There is indeed a danger that the very concept of love, even the word itself, might fade and disappear. It is no accident that love was the thing that excited and aroused the youth in the sixties. There was a revolt against lack of love, against the trivialization of love. Let's love one another, they said. But their promiscuity created a state of mind such that now there is a revolt against their revolt. There is a very real danger that love might fade away, for everything happens far too quickly these days.

If you read the novels of American and European literature before the sixties, you find that the initial gestures of encounter were beautiful, exalting, and agonizing. The boy looks at the girl and blushes; she blushes in turn. It takes him time to work up the courage to speak, and when he does, he stammers. It used to take months. But today all that is gone. A boy meets a girl and five minutes later they're in bed. Where is the love in that? It is a complete devaluation of love.

A sort of idolatry of the body and of sex?

Idolatry of the body, yes. Instant gratification. Everything has to be satisfied on the spot.

A famous passage in the Talmud recounts a scene in which three hakhamim *are discussing which verse in the Torah contains all the rest. Ben Zoma cites the verse:* Shma Israel, adonoi elohainu, adonoi ehod, *"Hear, O Israel, the Lord thy God, the Lord is One." Ben Nanas cites another:* veahavta lereakha kamokha, *"You shall love your neighbor as yourself." Finally Ben Pazi: "You shall sacrifice a lamb in the morning and another in the evening." After which Rabbi, their Master, declares: "the Torah is according to Ben Pazi." Didn't Rabbi Akiba hold that the mitzvah "love your neighbor" was actually the greatest?*

What is the meaning of Rabbi's answer?

What a beautiful passage that is! It's a kind of game, in the magical sense of the word. Each one asks, How can we find a single phrase, a single verse, that contains all the others? How can the microcosm contain the whole? And each one has a different answer. The sacrifice represents the physical effort of going to the Temple to participate in a rite. The verse "you shall love your neighbor as yourself" means something else: the most important thing is to know others, even before knowing God or the Temple. Finally, the third verse represents not an act, but spirituality. Each of the three sages has a theory, a very particular vision of the totality of Judaism. But that does not mean that each accepts only his own verse. On the contrary, they follow all the Torah's precepts and are wedded to all its words.

Isn't it curious that the injunction "Love your neighbor" is not explicitly included in the Ten Commandments, the aseret hadivrot, *pronounced by the Lord on Sinai?*

But you have the verse: *Lo tirtzah,* You shall not murder.

But that is a negative injunction, not a positive commandment like the one Levinas cites: "You shall love . . . "

Each of the Ten Commandments, except the first, deals with human relations.

But in terms of ethics more than in terms of love. . . .

In terms of emotion, yes. Except the first: *anokhi adoshem elohaikha,* I am the Lord thy God. This commandment is different. Moreover, according to the Talmud, it was the only commandment actually spoken by God. It was Moses who repeated the others. In fact, God spoke only the single word *anokhi,* I am. To my mind, the beauty of the Ten Commandments is precisely that all of them, except the one that begins *anokhi,* deal with human relations and not with the relation between man and God. Take them one by one. *Lo tirtzah,* You shall not murder. *Lo tinaph,* You shall not commit adultery. *Lo tignov,* You shall not steal. *Lo taanai vreakha ed shaker,* You shall not bear false witness against your neighbor. *Lo takhmod*, You shall not covet. . . .

The presence of others is always implicit, even in the commandment: You shall not make idols or graven images. What does this mean? Simply that such action is insulting to whoever sees you do it, so think of others! In the Torah the word *veahavta*, you shall love, occurs only three times: *veahavta et adoshem elohaikha*, You shall love your God Eternal with all your heart, all your soul, all your power. You shall love your neighbor as yourself. And finally: You shall love the stranger.

There is a logical sequence in these three verses. The sense is that if you love the stranger, then you will love your friend, and if you love your friend, then you will love God. One without the other—without the two others—would be an incomplete love.

Might this also mean that one must love one's enemy?

No, "You shall love your enemy" is not written.

The Torah, the Bible, knows the limits of the human heart. You must not go too far. One does not forgive one's enemy, unless he asks one's forgiveness. We do not have to love our enemy. Why should we? He seeks only to kill us. To love him would be unnatural.

Why is it that many Christians, even today, contrast the supposedly vengeful, merciless God of the "Old Testament"— which, as Martin Buber said, is actually neither old nor a testament—with the compassionate God of the New?

Because they don't really know the Bible. They don't know it in depth; they have read it badly, interpreted it poorly. For us there is no such thing as the "Old Testament." Buber was right to protest against that appellation. It's the Bible, not a testament. "The Bible" means "the Book," the book of life. To see God as vengeful is to betray a complete lack of understanding of Scripture, of its underlying passion, and of the generosity that radiates from it.

Does this lack of understanding also reflect a falsification of the Jewish Word and of the tradition of Israel as such?

It certainly does, and that is very serious. And sad too.

Are figures such as Mother Teresa and the Abbot Pierre of no concern to us? Do they not call out to us?

They do. I know Mother Teresa. What she is doing is admirable. I have never met the Abbot Pierre, but his activities, too, are noble and useful.

They are people who raise questions, and who force us to ask questions of ourselves.

And who act, too. It would be good if we had rabbis like them.

That is something I often think about. How do you explain the fact that there are no such figures in the history of the Jewish tradition, steeped as it is in the teachings of the Torah, in ethics and love for one's neighbor? Is it because of the often tragic conditions of the Jews in the Diaspora during the past twenty centuries, or does it have to do with the nature of Judaism itself?

It is a result of the ordeals which, true enough, have created a kind of second nature of Judaism. It was not easy to live in exile, in Diaspora, for nearly two thousand years. It was not easy to be born in exile, to bear children in exile, to know that you would die in exile. It was not easy to have to build on ruins constantly.

Nor to show great concern for others, particularly when others were so often our enemies. . . .

Precisely.

In Messengers of God *you wrote: "to watch over a man in pain is more urgent than to contemplate God." But isn't that exactly what contemplating God means to a believer: to live in the path of He who had His prophet say, "He recognized the orphan and the poor and He saw that it was good. That is surely what it is to know me"?*

Of course. But that is not the reason we have to do it. We must do it because a child is thirsty, because a friend is hungry. When I come to that child's aid, I place myself on a certain path, in a certain light. But the reason I must help the orphan is not because I have read that verse of the prophets, but because he is defenseless, and I must aid the child because he is in pain, or because his mother is sick, or because his parents are poor. When I grant such aid and succor, my act draws me closer to the call of the prophets, for God in His Scripture speaks to everyone, myself included. But I repeat, I must try to do good not simply because it is written, but also because it is a human duty, and we cannot shun that which is human. The Bible, in fact, only makes explicit what we must do.

Second Day

But what kind of world is it? No eyes are open, just as no stars have shined since a yellow star marked the death of countless innocents, and base violence and torture shamelessly defied the daylight.

Edmond Jabes

The Hurban

Philippe de Saint-Cheron: *Yesterday you said that you had survived only by chance. But you also said, paradoxically, that the birth, and thereby the life, of every person is in God's hands and is therefore not the product of chance. How is it that chance and its absence can both be inherent in certain circumstances of life?*

Elie Wiesel: Because I consider the Shoah a unique and exceptional event.

Do you mean that chance alone was decisive in the Event?

Words fail us when it comes to the Event.

Even providence disappeared during the Shoah. . . .

It is inapplicable. I find it inconceivable that God could have treated the souls of women, men, and children that way.
Perhaps you are familiar with the powerful question the Talmud reports Rabbi Yoshua Ben Levi as having asked the Prophet Elias: What was the Lord doing while we were talking?
What does He do while certain things are happening?
I am obsessed with that question. What was God doing while His children were being massacred by others of His children? After all, the others were children of God too, weren't they?

Don't you think that this impossibility of relying on provi-dence persisted afterward? Doesn't what happened in Cambo-dia or Vietnam also testify to the absurdity of the hatred—the chance—that kills hundreds of thousands of children?

One could certainly say so, provided one does not equate the two. But the question remains valid.

Given the death of a child—or of thousands of children, whether in Cambodia or elsewhere—how can you reconcile the absence of chance in birth, which is willed by God, with the chance of death?

I don't reconcile anything. But what was done in Cam-bodia, after all, was done by human beings. And the Shoah? Yes, human beings did that too. In that sense there is a point of comparison. Every tragedy involves more than its own immediate participants. But Auschwitz—that was different.

By that you mean that the Shoah had a greater religious or metaphysical significance than the other tragedies of history?

Auschwitz is conceivable neither without God nor with Him.

Perhaps these other catastrophes lack the explicit reference to God that is given by Israel. . . .

They are different, but I recognize the right of a Cam-bodian to say about Cambodia what I have said about Auschwitz.

Was the Shoah a moment in the Sacred History of Israel?

Yes. Catastrophe is part of Israel's history.

You once said, "For me to have lived, someone else had to die." Why do you think that your life must be linked to another's death?

Because I try to be honest with myself and to look unflinchingly into the depths of my own history and being. The fact is that the enemy was counting corpses at the time; he needed a thousand people one day, two thousand the next.

Even at the end?

Yes, even at the end. They were keeping count. And since I was not among those who died, someone else had to be.

What was it about the call of life that proved stronger than the abyss, even in your moments of doubt or despair?

I don't know. No one thing was stronger than anything else. There are fine-sounding phrases, like "the will to live," or to survive, or to testify. But for me it was nothing like that. As I said before, it was only by chance that I happened to live. It would be too much to say that I did anything to bring about my own survival, or that something inside me wanted to live. The truth is that after my father died, I felt only emptiness and nothingness.

Did you learn anything about man in the camp?

I learned that evil, like good, is infinite, and that the two are combined in man.

Did the people who endured the ordeal emerge with a new message and new strength?

Here again, it would be too optimistic to put it that way. Some emerged from the hell with a message of hope, while others chose a cry of despair. And if it turns out that new Hiroshimas are the consequence and result of Auschwitz, then we could well say just the opposite: that the message of Auschwitz was a total, definitive, and final Auschwitz. I don't want to generalize. We have no right to generalize or oversimplify.

Does the Event have a hermeneutic significance such that the Torah—and indeed all of Western philosophy and theology—must be reconsidered or reread?

It is a turning point that requires that everything be reevaluated. The entire past must be reconsidered.

Would you agree with Yankelovich that "forgiveness died in Auschwitz"?

Everything died in Auschwitz, in every way. But it depends on what sort of forgiveness you're talking about, and of whom it is asked. Otherwise the question is too general, too schematic. As I said yesterday, as far as the murderers are concerned, forgiveness is neither dead nor alive. It is not something that belongs to us. But forgiveness of man by man still exists today. Why wouldn't it? On the eve of Yom Kippur, the Law obliges me to forgive others: my friends, my fellows, even my enemies, provided that their acts do not go beyond my own person. But I must forgive them only if they ask forgiveness. In that case I am obliged to grant it.

In The Tragic Sense of Life *Miguel de Unamuno, speaking of those who do evil, writes, "Father, forgive them, for they know not what they do." But in his book* Pardonner?, *Yankelovich says about the Nazi hangmen, "Do not forgive them, for they knew very well what they were doing." What would your view be?*

I really don't think God needs my advice. He does what He wills. The problem of the Shoah is not whether or not to forgive, but something else entirely. I could not possibly describe it in one word, for no single word could explain or analyze, comprehend or convey, its horror and complexity.

Yet your message is one that subdues the drive for death and vengeance.

What would be the point of vengeance? Vengeance is idiotic, and hatred even more so.

Your message is one of love and peace, then?

Not of love, I don't think. But certainly of faith, and most of all of brotherhood and friendship.

In A Beggar in Jerusalem *you wrote the story of a young Jew who is murdered by the executioners during the war but does not die because he must stay alive to bear witness. Aren't you that same survivor who speaks out, who combats forgetfulness and insists on the specificity of Jewish martyrdom, who rises up in indignation against those who "revise" history, and who so often fears that he will not be heard?*

Yes, I certainly am.

Nearly all your books feature someone who should have been killed, who ought to be dead, but who does not die and instead returns.

That's true. When I talk about myself, as I am doing here, I am also speaking of all the survivors, and by extension of all men. But it's true that it is on the basis of my own personal and individual commitment that I attempt to rise ever higher so as to speak of others as well.

How have the Jews had the strength to remain Jewish through two thousand years of exodus, crossing the deserts of the nations and repeatedly suffering their hatred?

That is the great mystery. How have we managed to stay alive through history? Who kept us alive? We see the Torah, the Word of God, as living and eternal. That Word has given meaning to our own eternity, which emerges from us and returns to us. Other peoples have been stronger and richer than us, more powerful and more crafty. Strength and awareness of superiority were on their side. And yet . . . And not all the communities did survive: some assimilated, while others were massacred. Were it not for all the massacres throughout these twenty centuries, perhaps there would be hundreds of millions of Jews in the world today, as there are Chinese. But we have faced trials, assimilation, conversion. Every possible method has been used to kill the Jews, and there is not a single country in which the Jews have not been massacred, persecuted, at one time or another.

Doesn't history show that peoples who suffer cruel ordeals find a resilience within themselves and that their strength, stubbornness, and vitality rise commensurately with their trials?

Yes, but then how do you explain the disappearance of the ancient empires? At the end of the empire, Rome went through a very difficult period. The same for Pharaonic Egypt, Babylonia, the Venetian Republic, and so on.

It is true that the end of the Roman Empire was marked by decadence.

The empire suffered defeat and disaster, yet it did not survive. No, I don't think that misfortune is the cause of our survival. It was something else entirely, most especially the mission we have assumed and that we proclaim, the mission of Israel.

Do you think that Yom ha Shoah — *the day of commemoration of the Shoah — will or should remain a day of religious mourning like Tisha b'Ab, the ninth day of the month of Ab, the anniversary of the destruction of the two Temples of Jerusalem? Or could it someday be combined with Tisha b'Ab, for example?*

No. Begin tried to combine the two. He was under pressure from certain American orthodox rabbis who, for religious reasons, quite naturally feel uncomfortable with the Shoah. They asked Begin to change the date of Yom ha Shoah to coincide with Tisha b'Ab. But that could not be done, and it will not be done, because Yom ha Shoah is a day apart. It cannot be reduced to anything else in the whole history of Israel. And so it will be until the end of time.

Don't you think that this day has a different significance depending on whether we spend it in Eretz Israel or in the Diaspora, and that young Israelis may feel less concerned by it than young European or American Jews?

That is exactly why it is so important in Israel. When President Carter appointed me chairman of the Presidential Commission on the Holocaust, I set two conditions. First, that we have a national ceremony, in Congress or the White House. Second, that the date coincide with the Israeli date every year. This drove the

officials in Washington crazy, because our calendars
rarely coincide. They didn't understand, and I had to in-
sist. Now the ceremony is held every year on kafzain Nisan [the twenty-seventh day of the month of Nisan, the
first month of the Jewish year, the month of the Exodus
from Egypt], and the president or vice president always
accompanies the high state dignitaries. I am very happy
to have brought this about and that it will continue. On
the same day, the governors in all fifty states organize a
ceremony like the one in Washington. All fifty states
therefore participate in the demonstrations to com-
memorate the victims of the Shoah.

*Don't those Jews who now embody the living community of
Israel, the people of the Covenant, also embody the living
Temple?*

Every human being is a living temple. Every Jew who
contemplates the Temple, who recalls the Temple, and
who prays for its reconstruction is its high priest.

*In a sense, the Temple was destroyed six million
times. . . .*

I believe I have put it just that way myself. It was the
worst catastrophe in Jewish history. When I try to think
of a word to use to designate it, I prefer hurban [whirl-
wind], which also evokes the destruction of the Temple.
That is what we ought to call the Jewish Catastrophe.
Just after the war, whenever two Jews met, they would
speak not of the Holocaust—that word had not yet entered the language—nor of the Shoah, but of the Hurban: "Where were you during the Hurban? What did
you do during the Hurban?" *Hurban* was the word that
dominated the language and thoughts of the survivors.
    That is what Hurban is: destruction, total destruction.
The word places us within a history: the first destruc-

tion, the second, and the third. Just because it's a little hard to pronounce in French, that's no reason not to use it.

If you read Yiddish poems and memoirs of the Catastrophe, you will find that *hurban* is the word used by religious poets and secular chroniclers alike. In France Manès Sperber also used it in a very moving essay. And rightly so, for he had a finely honed sense of language and history.

Can we say that the enormity of the Event you experienced is comparable to the Exodus from Egypt?

Personally I compare it to something even greater: the Revelation on Mount Sinai. It was a kind of anti-revelation.

Fackenheim has referred to this comparison you have made between the Revelation of Sinai and the revelation of Auschwitz. . . .

It was an anti-revelation, in the sense that everything this Event revealed was anti-something: anti-Messiah, anti-good, anti-life. It was not simply death, but something more. A genuine antinomian process.

Delving deeper into my question: in the messianic sense, can the Hurban be considered the negative pole of what is symbolized by the Exodus from Egypt?

Absolutely. That's why I sometimes use images from the world of my childhood. The gathering of exiles, for example. The night of our arrival in the camp was a kind of gathering of exiles. The images, of course, were mystical and anti-redemptive. I thought that the Messiah had come.

The Messiah of death.

Yes, the Messiah of death. The malefic pole, the destroyer pole.

It is as if God once descended among men, His creatures, in order to save them, but since the destruction of the Second Temple, in the year 70 of our era, it is man who has tried to ascend, to raise himself up as though to save God.

That is a very beautiful mystical Hasidic thought. In mysticism, man alone is capable of bringing about the advent the Messiah, of freeing humanity from its chains and of freeing God from His prison, the *shekhina* of His pain. [*Shekhina* is the presence of God on earth.] In that sense we act *for* God. We always ask God to take pity on us, a great Hasidic master once said, but when will we take pity on God?

How is it that, having foreseen everything in His eternal present, the Blessed Holy One still left man free? That seems a great mystery.

It is the mystery of man, the mystery of God in the life of man.

If we follow this thought through, we might say that the Messiah whom we await is a man, but the man most completely in the Lord's image. What must save man is the human in him—which is to say, his divine component—and not God's intervention.

Yes, it is man who must save man. That is the price of the freedom God has given us. This freedom itself, of course, comes from God, but it is up to man to lay claim to it.

I would like to go back to the subject of one of my first questions, theodicy. Doesn't theodicy imply that we must think of suffering, of Evil, as related to sin? Isn't Job—along with Isaac—the very paradigm of any refutation of theodicy? Doesn't the great theological protest of which you speak in Paroles d'étranger *signify a radical cleavage between evil and compassion, between evil and meaning?*

Job does speak of this. He says that there was punishment without sin. And if there was punishment without sin, does that mean that there was also sin without punishment? I once said—smilingly—to my teacher Saul Lieberman: I believe that the *tzadik*, the Just Man, never receives recompense, whereas the evil and impious are always punished. It may take time, but punishment will come. The impious never remain unpunished. We must uphold this conviction even in the case of the Shoah: the Just never received recompense, because no recompense is possible. But is there a punishment? The only punishment commensurate with the crime would be the destruction of the world. And we are coming nearer to that.

That is a very pessimistic, tragic vision.

Pessimistic, yes. But if we are conscious of this pessimism, perhaps we will be capable of warding off catastrophe.

In our modern societies, evil is essentially disease. In the Torah, disease is often interpreted as punishment from God. Do you accept this relationship, particularly in regard to sexually transmitted diseases? Is it not both indecent and outrageous to associate AIDS with sin, as some dare to do today?

Yes, it is outrageous. It is absolutely inadmissible and unacceptable to say that AIDS is a consequence of sin.

It is shameful to toy with human misery and to exploit human suffering for political—or worse, religious—purposes. I am outraged and hurt that some people dare to say such things.

Returning to the Bible, how do you reconcile disease with the idea of punishment? How can we accept this relation of cause and effect?

I do not regard disease as punishment. In the Bible, only certain diseases are regarded as punishments from heaven. An example would be the punishment of Miriam, who cursed her brother Moses. But not all diseases are punishment. They are a part of life, of man's existence, of the body's fragility. Most of all, in the Bible every disease has a spiritual dimension. It is the Cohen, the priest, who cares for the sick, precisely because of this spiritual dimension.

The two things that unite people most strongly today are the struggle against disease and the struggle against atomic destruction, don't you think?

In fact, people are united by both good and evil. They are united in wartime, for instance. But for what purpose? To destroy, to kill, to massacre. And also to survive.

Isn't disease a kind of battle within the body, a battle of nature against life, of death against life?

I am neither a doctor nor a researcher. But in any event, I refuse to bring God into disease by claiming that He causes it in order to punish us. Some other religious Jews—with whom I do not agree at all—say that the Maalot tragedy occurred because the *mezuzot* on the doors were not kosher. [A *mezuzah* is a small case containing a parchment of the Shma Israel which Jews attach to their door frames.] An outrageous explanation. I also heard somewhere—though I hope it is not true—that one or several rabbis have claimed that the Shoah occurred so as to prevent the Jews from assimilating, which is just as offensive as to condemn the Zionist movement by claiming that the Shoah was necessary for the birth of Israel. As if the creation of Israel were a response to the Shoah! I do not accept this "response." I would not like to heap such guilt upon young Israelis, who might then say: six million Jews had to die that I might be free! Personally, I prefer to think of these as separate, irreducible, and inescapable mysteries.

Péguy has written: "Lost suffering is the greatest mystery of creation." Do you think that futile suffering is the greatest incomprehensible mystery for a believer?

Not the greatest, but certainly one of the great mysteries of creation. All this suffering might potentially arouse a new sensitivity. If it were lost—if no poem, message, or promise came of it—that would be horrible. The irreparable loss would be doubled. But simply to say that lost suffering is *the greatest* mystery? . . . As you know, I get very suspicious whenever someone says "the greatest." Who knows what *the* greatest is? I am fairly sure that even Péguy might well have written something different at another time. At that particular moment in his life, at that instant of his existence, that's what he thought.

Do you think that today—after Auschwitz, after the paroxysm of the Passion of Israel—it is possible to contemplate the religions of the Book without taking account of the theological question of Evil?

This Event obviously compels self-reevaluation, though this concerns the Jewish and Christian religions much more than Islam, because in fact Islam was far removed from everything that happened. But Christianity cannot avoid taking account of the Shoah.

Have we not arrived at a moment in history at which the believer can no longer put forward proof of God's existence, as Descartes did, for example?

I have never been able to take such proofs seriously. It is all very well for philosophers, but not for believers. You know the famous Hasidic saying: "For the believer there are no questions, for the atheist there are no answers."

What I mean is that the Hurban does not prove Descartes right or wrong. Descartes is right or wrong in relation to philosophy in general and his own philosophy in particular.

The Hurban, however, goes far deeper than simply challenging these philosophical proofs. The Hurban challenged the faith of the believers, not of the unbelievers. Descartes, like Pascal, was addressing unbelievers, infidels. Hence his value, and also his weakness.

Judeo-Christian Relations

Philippe de Saint-Cheron: *In* A Beggar in Jerusalem *you had this to say about Jesus: "It is not you who will die for us, but we who will die for you." How do you perceive the Christian message? Are the Jews still genuinely threatened by persistent anti-Semitism among some Christians and by the missionary character of the Catholic Church?*

Elie Wiesel: In *A Beggar in Jerusalem* I spoke of Jesus sincerely, with considerable compassion and even pity. I suggested that he did not know, that he could not have known, what his disciples would do in his name, and that had he been aware of all the crimes men would later commit in his name and all the blood they would spill, supposedly for him, he would have regretted it. The sense of the passage you cited was: you are not going to die for us; we are going to die because of you. Today, whenever anyone is in danger, we are in danger too. When Jews are afraid, I owe it to them to believe that their fear is justified. And since there are many Jews who still believe that there is a threat of anti-Semitism, it is my duty to accept their fear.

On the other hand, the efforts undertaken by liberal Christians — Catholics and Protestants alike — must be acknowledged. It is very important that there is a liberal movement within the churches that is doing all it can to bring about a rapprochement with Judaism and the Jews. This movement is very strong here in the United

65

States and in France too. Yet it is a minority within the Christian community, and we Jews therefore have a duty to draw closer to these men and women, to make our affection and gratitude clear to them. They are a minority among their own, just as we are a minority in the eyes of the entire world.

But you ask whether there is danger. I would say, Yes, there is. There is always danger, especially in the event of an economic downturn or a rise in unemployment. If that happens, then reactionaries will look for a scapegoat: it's because of the Jews, they will say. So there is a latent danger, although I do not think there could be another "holocaust," another Hurban. As long as we do not forget, we will be spared that danger. But threats and insecurity undoubtedly persist.

In our century some Christians have converted to Judaism, particularly since the Shoah and the creation of the State of Israel, even though Judaism has never sought converts—quite the contrary, in fact. Isn't the attraction to the Jewish people now arising among Christian consciences after twenty centuries of anti-Semitism a sign of a renewal of Israel's mission in the world?

No. As you said yourself, conversion has never been a way of life or mode of expression among us. If a proselyte persists in coming to us despite being discouraged, then we accept him with open arms, and he becomes a brother. Afterward, as you know very well from your own personal experience, all the rights, duties, and religious obligations, including consciousness and memory, become part and parcel of the commitment of the convert or, as in your case, of the Baal Teshuva. But to say that the mission of Israel is to seek converts is false.

I didn't mean that this was a mission of Israel, but rather that awareness of Israel's history has led certain Christians to convert to Judaism.

But let's not exaggerate. There are very few such cases. Don't forget that there are some four billion human beings on this earth. Even if a few thousand people have converted to Judaism in the past forty years, think what that represents. . . .

On the individual level, however, this consciousness does exist, and that is all to the good. The Talmud asks: "Why do we feel such love for the Guer, the foreigner? Because whereas the children of Israel were compelled to accept the Torah, the Guer comes to it voluntarily." When that happens, of course, we love him, but to say that there has been a revival of the mission of the Jews — a mission that never existed in the first place — or even a rise in callings, really I don't think so at all. Of course, the mystery of Israel, the history of Israel, has always exercised an attraction on some individuals, and sometimes even on entire peoples, such as the Khazars [a Turkic people between the Volga and the Dnieper who converted to Judaism in the middle of the eighth century]. Some individuals have come to us out of generosity or sadness, or out of compassion, or out of friendship, need, or need for friendship, and they have adopted a people with a very sharp sense of friendship and a powerful sense of memory.

How do you explain the fact that as late as 1987 a renowned Catholic author could write something like this: "We have moved from the Old Testament to the New Testament. The older version seems to depict God as merciless, unjust, and cruel, for He ordained that the sins of the fathers be visited upon the sons. This God of unjust justice must be replaced by the image of a just God full of merciful love for the weaknesses of His creatures."

What accounts for such bad faith, such blindness?

Who wrote that?

Jean Guitton.

Well, you know, he is only repeating what others have said and written before him, beginning with the Church Fathers themselves.

But it's dreadful that anyone would dare to write such lies after Auschwitz, after what happened in Christian Europe between 1933 and 1945.

Yes, it is dreadful. It proves that he does not understand the Bible correctly, and that he knows even less about the talmudic commentaries. He could not possibly know them.

But shouldn't such knowledge be a special responsibility for a renowned Catholic writer and a member of the French Academy to boot?

He wrote a very good book on Bergson, too. In the Talmud, Ezekiel is chided for having said that the sins of the fathers are not visited upon the sons, but that each person is judged according to his own virtues. For us, Ezekiel is as important as the Torah. He is the prophet of exile, of suffering and promise. I hope that Jean Guitton's readers will nevertheless be able to recognize the truth.

Commenting on Yuri-Zwi Grinberg's poem "They Have Murdered Their God," you wrote in Paroles d'étranger: *"by trying to kill the Jews, the Christians killed their God." Do you think that Christian anti-Semitism bears a great responsibility for the Nazi lunacy (while not forgetting, of course, the many Christians—laymen, priests, and religious Catholics, as well*

*as Protestants and members of the Orthodox Church—who
protected Jews during the war, sometimes at the cost of their
own lives)?*

There was, of course, a magnificent, marvelous
minority: the *tzadikai oumot-haolam*, the Just among the
nations, who risked or even sacrificed their own lives
and the lives of their families to save Jews. To them we
are eternally grateful. But at the same time, no historian,
no researcher, no thinker, no honest religious person
would now deny the Christian influence on Nazi anti-
Semitic theory. Sometimes we find an identical archetypical fanaticism. Without the foundation afforded by
Christianity, Nazi anti-Semitism would not have attained the violence that it did, nor the paroxysm of hatred and murder.

*Have you ever met John Paul II? Do you feel an affinity for
his great moral choices, his warnings, his constant appeals to
inalienable human values, and his concern for interreligious
dialogue?*

I have never met John Paul II. Some of his speeches
have moved me, especially those that talk of poverty,
misery, oppression, freedom, and human rights in Poland or in the countries of the Third World. On the other
hand, I am somewhat suspicious of the stance he has
taken on the Shoah, in public at least. To begin with, in
1979 he went to Auschwitz. He meditated in Maximilian
Kolbe's cell and referred to Edith Stein. But he made no
explicit mention of the Jews who were killed in Auschwitz and Birkenau. He spoke only of the "people whose
sons and daughters were condemned to extermination."
Why didn't he say: "the Jews"?
Second, he celebrated mass in Birkenau. I find that insensitive, because the Jews who died in Auschwitz-
Birkenau were among the most pious in Europe.

He should have taken a rabbi and nine Jewish men with him and told them to say Kaddish for the Jewish victims while he celebrated mass for the Catholics. What was he trying to do? Convert the Jews posthumously? The mass is the most Catholic of all services, and that's why I think it was hurtful of him to celebrate a mass for all the victims and therefore for the Jews as well.

Third, look at this business with Waldheim. He never should have met with Waldheim; he could have avoided it, if necessary even by stalling and temporizing. Last week he went to Maidenek, and here again—according to the report in *Libération*—he mentioned fourteen nationalities. Everyone knows that at least 90 percent of the victims were Jews, yet he did not mention the Jews in Maidenek. If I consider all this in its context, it is only natural for me to be suspicious. And then there is Israel. The fact that he has still not recognized the State of Israel is an unfriendly act toward the Jewish people.

What about the beatification of Edith Stein?

Edith Stein was a convert who, after all, was killed not because she was a Christian but because she was a Jew. But once again the arrow points in a certain direction.

Is he perhaps less open-minded than he appears to be?

Socially, he is open-minded.

But isn't he much closer to the Jews than Paul VI, who did not even speak the words "Israel" or "Jew" when he went to Israel? That was quite a feat!

That's something else again, because Paul VI even defended the memory of Pius XII in Israel. And what was the meaning of his refusal to enter Israel by way of Jerusalem? I think Israel was wrong to receive him as it did. A special gateway was installed for the pope in Jericho.

I have heard, however, that Pius XII did save many Jews during the war.

Probably several hundred Italian Jews, but that's not the point. A single word from him could have saved so many others. But he never spoke that word.

Which brings us back to the relation between speech and silence.

Exactly. But don't forget that François Mauriac criticized Pius XII for this well before Rolf Hochhuth or anyone else.

It took nearly twenty centuries of Christian anti-Semitism, up to the conflagration of Auschwitz, before the Jewish Word was finally heard and recognized not as a mere fossil but, in the best of cases, as an equal message, or at least as a living, contemporary one and not merely some sort of remnant. Nevertheless, some Christians—in particular some Catholics—miss no opportunity to point out that while they are pleased that we are no longer accused of deicide, they are less content that the Carmelites, for example, are being forced out of Auschwitz by Jewish protest. Doesn't this show a strange cleavage between some Christians' willingness to absolve the Jews of responsibility for the death of Jesus on the one hand and their unwillingness, on the other hand, to hear any talk of Christian responsibility for the long history of anti-Semitism in general and for the Shoah in particular?

I am not sure that these two phenomena are linked. Personally, I prefer to hear Christians themselves talk about Christian responsibility in the Shoah. Coming from us, it hurts them. I know sincere Christians who were pained, saddened, and appalled by this Event. When they speak of it, they strike a different tone. But to leap from that to the claim that we Jews ought not to speak of it is absurd. Who has a greater right to speak than the victims, the survivors? We were the victims, and that's why we have not only the right but the duty to talk about it. Nevertheless, I prefer that it be Christians who bring up the role of Christianity in our tragedy.

But don't you find it curious that some Christians rose up against the Jewish protest about the business of the Carmelites in Auschwitz?

Yes, I do. I myself was part of that protest. I wrote on the subject. The reactions? Some said, We'll take care of this for you, let us handle it, it's our problem, a Catholic problem, and we will resolve it.

I respect that attitude. Others said, You have no right to interfere in this project. But we must continue to protest.

This shows that despite the good will and the undeniably more open attitude within the Church today, there is still resistance. . . .

There is a reactionary wing, even in the Vatican itself. On the other hand, I know three cardinals intimately who are quite open to our concerns, anxieties, and aspirations.

What was your reaction to the naming of Cardinal Lustiger as archbishop of Paris? I believe you know him well.

I met him only afterward, once he had already become the archbishop of Paris. Since then we have established very close ties. He is undoubtedly one of the best men of peace in the Church today. As a Jew, and as his friend,

I have no wish to hurt him, but I nevertheless regret that he did not remain Jewish, that he did not become what he could have become within the Jewish people. He converted at a very early age, and I am convinced that had he met a rabbi instead of a priest at the time when his need for religion first arose, he would have become a great Jewish scholar.

In fact, he had no experience of Judaism in his childhood and adolescence, discovering it only as an adult, when he had already joined the Church.

His parents were not religious. They were secular, even atheists, and he took his first steps toward religion under the influence of a priest. Had he instead encountered a Jewish chaplain in high school or at the university, he would now be bearing a share of Jewish responsibility.

Another great Catholic figure in France is Cardinal Decourtray. Do you know him?

I met him in Lyon when I went to testify at the Barbie trial. I visited him and the grand rabbi. I was very impressed with Cardinal Decourtray. He is a man of complete integrity—totally open-minded and thoroughly compassionate—and at the same time he is rigorous in his thought and behavior. I like him very much.

Earlier you mentioned François Mauriac, and I would like to come back to him for a moment. There is a very astonishing sentence about you in his notebooks: "Elie Wiesel has a most singular understanding of Jesus," seeing him "as a pious, law-abiding Jew who did not die, for in dying he became God." And he adds: "Elie Wiesel stands at the border between the two Testaments."

I know you have great admiration for Mauriac, but hasn't

his faith caused him to distort your views in this case?

That may be his perception of me, but I have never stood "at the border of the New Testament." I respect Christians who are attached to the New Testament, provided that they respect my attachment to our Bible, to the *Tanakh*.

Could you tell me about your visit to the Stockholm cathedral when you were awarded the Nobel Prize?

It is customary for the Nobel laureate to deliver a speech for peace at the Stockholm cathedral. So I went. Usually this is a solemn ceremony, but it so happens that the archbishop of the cathedral is an old friend of mine. It was a peace service, not a religious service. In my speech from the pulpit I stressed three points:

"The friendship between us is too close for me not to tell you what I feel. You cannot expect a Jew like me to check his memories at the door. When I come inside, my memory comes with me.

"There was a time when a Jew entered a cathedral only to emerge a Christian, and I hope that you did not expect me to convert.

"Nevertheless, the fact that you have invited me and that I now stand here, in this pulpit, telling you these things as a Jew and speaking as a Jew to a non-Jewish audience, in the name of peace and for peace, shows that there has been a change. When I was young, I avoided church doors, crossing the street so as not to pass by them. Today I stand here in this cathedral as a Jew."

Do you ever find yourself thinking, as Kafka did, that the Messiah will come not on the last day but on the day after the last?

I love Kafka. There is such power in everything he
wrote! That is a magnificent phrase, sober and somber.
Sometimes I think that we are condemned to wait without end, that we Jews live in suspension, that when the
waiting is over, we will have to wait yet again, that even
after the last day, there will be yet another day, the last
of the last, the post-ultimate.

*Aren't there also texts in our tradition that say that it is the
Messiah who waits for man?*

We proclaim it. In fact, there are many beautiful images depicting the Messiah at the gates of Rome.

Why Rome?

Because at the time Rome was the opposite of Jerusalem. Other images depict the Messiah in an eagle's nest
or in the *pardes*, the orchard of knowledge. But it is always the Messiah who is waiting to be called. He waits
for man's summons.

Is the pardes *an allegory for paradise?*

In some texts it represents paradise, in others the orchard of knowledge.

*Is messianism the business of the Messiah alone, or of man
as well?*

Both. It is a human initiative, but above all else an
offering. It is first of all God's gift to man and secondly
Israel's gift to the other nations. Messianism is a Jewish
idea. You will find no messianic idea elsewhere. Messianism must therefore be seen as an offering, a promise.

Some Writers Deal with Evil

Philippe de Saint-Cheron: *Which writers, particularly of the past century, have had the greatest impact on you?*

Elie Wiesel: First of all Dostoyevsky, for whom Evil was the dominant subject, and Kafka, and Thomas Mann, especially *The Magic Mountain*. In France, Malraux, Mauriac, and Camus have been important to me.

What about Miguel de Unamuno?

Yes, very much so, though at a different level. Of Unamuno's works I prefer not so much the novels, but essentially *The Tragic Sense of Life* and *The Life of Don Quixote and Sancho Panza*.

It seems to me that his perception of the agony of faith—in the etymological sense of agonia, *meaning "struggle," or "combat"—and his terrible ordeal of doubt and inner darkness make him one of the most important thinkers of our time, even though he died back in 1936, during the early months of the war in Spain. Yet he is little known and even largely forgotten today—except in his own country, of course. In France one rarely hears his name, and he is read by only a few students. Isn't your agony of faith close to his in some sense?*

Close, but different, for mine is firmly situated within Judaism. On the other hand, who knows but what Una-

76

muno was of Sephardic descent. In any case, he was close to us. He had that great anxiety.

It is indeed a pity that he is so little known today. He ought to be reread, rediscovered, and studied, especially for the courage he displayed in 1936. In *The Testament* I quote his speech at the University of Salamanca, delivered in the presence of a fascist general. "This university is a temple," he said.

*   *   *

On October 12, 1936, at the beginning of the civil war in Spain, General Millan Astray delivered a violent harangue against Catalonia and the Basque country at the University of Salamanca, where Unamuno was still rector.

The general spoke to a packed amphitheatre, and his audience chanted the horrible slogan of the fascist Legion: "Viva la muerte!" Unamuno then rose and spoke these words, his last as rector of the university, for on that very day he took refuge in his small apartment, where he died a few months later, on December 31, 1936:

"You are all waiting to see what I will say. You know me, and you know that I cannot keep silent. There are times when to keep silent is to lie, for silence can be interpreted as acquiescence. I would like to add something to General Millan Astray's speech, if one may call it that. I leave aside the personal insults of his invective against the Basques and the Catalonians. I myself was born in Bilbao. The bishop seated here beside me, whether he likes it or not, is a Catalonian from Barcelona. . . .

"As for the Communist atrocities on which they harp so endlessly, be advised that the most obscure militiawoman—though she be, as they say, a prostitute—fighting arms in hand and risking death for what she believes, is less mean in spirit than the women I saw leave our banquet yesterday evening, their bare arms caressed by flowers and precious cloth, to watch Marxists being brought before the firing squad. . . .

"I have just heard a morbid, senseless cry: Long live death! I who have spent my life creating paradoxes that have aroused the irritation of those who failed to grasp them must tell you, speaking as an expert, that this barbaric paradox is loathsome to me. . . . General Millan Astray is a cripple. I say that not out of discourtesy. Cervantes was a cripple too. But unfortunately, there are far too many cripples in Spain today. And there will be even more unless God comes to our aid. I tremble at the thought that General Millan Astray may lay the basis for a mass psychology. A cripple who lacks the spiritual grandeur of a Cervantes will normally seek solace in the mutilations he is able to inflict on those around him. . . . A Spain without Biscay and Catalonia would be a country like you, General, with one eye and one arm!"

General Millan Astray: "Death to intelligence! . . . Long live death!" Others in the audience take up his cry.

Unamuno: "This university is a temple to intelligence. Your words defile it. You will prevail because you possess more brute force than you need, but you will not convince. To convince you would need what you lack: reason and justice.

"I consider it futile to urge you to think of Spain. I have finished."

*   *   *

Philippe de Saint-Cheron: *Have you read* The Tragic Sense of Life *with your students?*

Elie Wiesel: No, I have not taught a course on that book alone. Usually I take a theme and study it in a dozen or so works. I always begin with the Bible, taking either a chapter or an entire book of Scripture. Then we follow the theme through the centuries. So I have touched on Unamuno's work, but perhaps someday I will give an entire course on him.

What do you think of Nietzsche? How do you interpret his conception of Judaism as a slave morality?

Nietzsche did not understand. As you may know, there is an anti-Semitic religious literature depicting the Jews as a diseased tribe of slaves who were driven out of Egypt precisely because they were infected with leprosy. The authors of this literature therefore regarded Jewish theology, Jewish morality, and Jewish philosophy as slave theology, morality, and philosophy. Such people understood nothing. Their aversion to the Jews was so great that they also detested the New Testament, which they saw as derived from the Bible. Otherwise they would have been good Christians. Since the New Testament was too close to the Bible, Nietzsche didn't like the Christians either. I think that his genius lies in form and style more than in content. He was a great poet more than a great philosopher.

When did you discover Nietzsche, and how did you perceive his cry, "God is dead"?

It is blasphemy—frivolous blasphemy, in fact. During the sixties, a philosophical school in the United States took up the "God is dead" theme. I found it offensive. Some of these philosophers even tried to lay claim to me, alleging that I had said it in *Night*. I had to straighten them out. When I was young, I explained, to say that God was alive one had first to go to the *mikvai* [the ritual bath, in Jewish tradition] to purify oneself so as to be worthy of the affirmation. Now they say "God is dead" and order a coffee as if that were all there was to it. Once upon a time the phrase must have really meant something. But now they speak such a phrase, act as if they had said nothing, and simply turn the page. I think it meant something to Nietzsche, who originated the cry:

it expressed his despair. But it never had any real reso-
nance for me.

I have noticed that in Beyond Good and Evil *Nietzsche
seems much closer to the Jews than to the Christians. He clearly preferred our Bible to the New Testament, which he considered a "monument to rococo taste." Greek and Hindu literature, he wrote, offer nothing comparable to the "Old
Testament."*

It is true that at various times he exhibited great passion for the Jews and for all they represented. But it is
undeniable that the Nazis made use of his teachings—
which proves that there was something in them capable
of being adapted for other ends. I am not saying that he
is responsible for what others made of his philosophy,
but his thought and work contain a fascination with the
superman, and that was attractive to the Nazis.

*Malraux said that Nietzsche was fiercely opposed to anti-
Semitism, calling it the worst possible thing.*

Yes, I've seen that phrase attributed to him. It was
primarily his sister who distorted his work, in particular
by entitling his last book *The Will to Power*.

Is Kafka the great contemporary writer of exile?

He is certainly one of the great ones. He was exiled
first of all in another language, secondly in a country not
his own, and finally within his own family and in his relations with women. He never found peace. No sooner
would he love one woman than he would fall in love
with another, as Kierkegaard did. He wrote in German,
but he would have liked to have expressed himself in
Yiddish. He lived in Prague, but he would have liked to

have lived in Palestine. And the problems with his father! Kafka was truly the visionary of exile.

*But was he really as we usually see him? Some contem-
porary critics have rejected what they call the "Kafka myth" of
despair and absurdity, of implacable law and omnipresent
guilt. Hannah Arendt, for example, argues that* The Castle
and The Trial *ought to be read as pure fiction, as depicting not
reality or possibility, but utopia. Is there another Kafka,
another—or even several other—possible readings of his work,
apart from the traditional interpretation?*

There are indeed a thousand and one possible readings of Kafka. He was a seminal author, and it is quite
natural that every reader, every interpreter, can find
whatever he wants in Kafka.

There are aberrant things too.

Definitely. For instance, there is a Zionist reading.
Max Brod, the man who rescued Kafka's work, claims
that taken as a whole, his books constitute a Zionist
parable. It's possible, why not? Max Brod himself lived
in Israel. Others, like Hannah Arendt, interpret it as a
utopia. As for the Marxists, they don't like Kafka, because his work corresponds to no Marxist theory and is
therefore anti-Marxist. All interpretations are possible
and arguable, even those that may appear aberrant. Because sometimes their authors have aberrant ideas.

*Kafka wrote somewhere: "In this brief and fleeting life, how
can we even . . . walk down a staircase? It's impossible! The
time allotted to you is so short that to lose a single second is
to lose your entire life, for that is how long your life lasts: exactly as long as the time you lose." Isn't this a very pessimistic
statement? How would you read it?*

Pessimistically. Pessimism is stronger than optimism in Kafka. But it's a biblical statement too, taken almost directly from Job. It was Job who said, "Man is but a shadow, and what is the life of a shadow?" A fleeting instant. In the Talmud, moreover, every minute counts. Every minute must be seen as life's first and last. Perhaps this is the last instant I have to change, to repent, to correct my ways. Kafka's statement stands firmly in the biblical spirit.

Wouldn't it be more optimistic, and perhaps more powerful, to say, "to gain a single second is to gain your entire life"?

It amounts to the same thing, but it is quite possible that he might have written the exact opposite at the next moment. The mirror can point both ways. In fact, you will find both forms in the Talmud. The treatise *'Avodah Zora* recounts that when Rabbi Yehuda Hanassi, the prince, saw the martyrdom of Rabbi Hanina ben Teradion, he wept and said: "There are men who win the world to come, the life to come, in a single hour, while others lose that life in the same hour." Rabbi Yehuda says both. If Kafka had been Rabbi Yehuda Hanassi, he too would have spoken both phrases.

André Malraux fought fascism all his life, from the war in Spain to the Bengali independence struggle in 1971, when he supported Bangladesh. His support for Israel was also constant, and he publicly condemned Israel's expulsion from the Unesco regional structures in 1974. He often evoked the Camps in his work and in his funeral speeches, such as the one he delivered for Jean Moulin or the one in Chartres on the thirtieth anniversary of the liberation of the Camps, a year before his death. But I have never understood why he was silent about the Shoah.

In one of my books I said that all great writers, Malraux among them, have felt this sense of propriety. Their silence is commendable. They may have written essays on the Shoah—some of them did, in fact—but they felt they had no right to talk about it in their novels. And I agree.

Malraux devotes the last chapter of his Antimémoires *to the Camps, practically without mentioning the Shoah. He raises just one question: "Were there other successful revolts besides that of the Jews of Treblinka?"*

I know that he wrote a magnificent preface to Sperber's moving book *Qu'une larme dans l'océan* and another to a volume of photographs entitled *Israel.* So he did comment, which clearly shows that he was shaken, upset, and pained by this catastrophe. I like Malraux well enough to rise to his defense.

It would have pained me had he written a novel—a bad novel—about the ordeal, as so many others have done.

Malraux often cited this memorable statement by a man coming out of prison: "There are only three books you can stand to read in prison: The Idiot, Don Quixote, *and* Robinson Crusoe.*" And Malraux added, "of these three authors, two— Cervantes and Dostoyevsky—were imprisoned, while the third, Daniel Defoe, was pilloried." If you had to answer that same question, what books would you cite?*

I would give a different answer. I would say the Bible, the Babylonian or Jerusalem Talmud (both if possible), and Maimonides.

When you returned, the first book you asked for when you got to the Maison d'enfants was the Talmud. . . .

Because they already had the Bible, but not the Talmud. We had only the Torah, which we needed, of
course, for the sabbath service. And there were prayer
books too.

Were all the children in this Maison d'enfants Jewish?

Yes, there were four hundred of us Jewish children in
Ecouis, in the Eure. We stayed there just a few weeks
and were then divided into two groups, religious and
nonreligious. I was in the religious group. About a hundred of us set out for Ambloy, near Vendôme. Then we
moved on to Taverny and then to Versailles. I spent
quite a lot of time in these children's homes. I directed
a choir there, and I also studied a lot, especially French,
which François Wahl taught me.

*I would like to ask you something else about writers and
Evil. Pierre Emmanuel thought that the imprisonment of
writers and poets in totalitarian countries did honor to the
word. In another sense, he also felt that the death sentence
against Brasillach after the war was equally as legitimate as the
death sentences against the direct executors of the Shoah, because for a writer, to speak is to act. Do you share that view?*

As I told you, I am against the death penalty as a matter of principle, so it is difficult for me to say yes. But if
I was for it—and I think that in certain cases I am—then
yes, I would agree. A committed writer like Brasillach,
who wrote violent anti-Semitic articles in *Je suis partout*,
had to be judged and condemned. You cannot say that
a writer has some special privilege just because all he
does is write. That should not afford him divine protec-
tion from the law.

On the contrary, he has an enormous responsibility.

Indeed, if the SS criminal is condemned to death, then it is natural that an intellectual who passionately incited ideological hatred and racism during the war should be condemned as well.

Do you draw a distinction between the artist or writer on the one hand and the man on the other? Can you enjoy the works of people like Wagner, Céline, or Brasillach, admiring them as creators regardless of their behavior and ideology?

Céline was a brilliant bastard. *Journey to the End of the Night* is a great book, and he was a great writer. Especially at the beginning. But then he lost his genius. His last books were not as good. That was his punishment: when he became an anti-Semite, he lost his talent. Blinded by stupid hatred, he turned mediocre, which he had not been earlier. I repeat, he was a bastard. No one has the right to write the things he did. It is criminal to endorse the Shoah, as he did in his articles and books.

Doesn't this odious attitude make it morally impermissible to read the works of these authors?

We ought to approach them as a whole, saying to ourselves: here is a book by an author who wrote masterpieces and then became an anti-Semite. The reader must have an overall view.

On several occasions you have made reference to your teacher Shushani, who also taught Levinas. But you have rarely spoken of Saul Lieberman, another of your teachers.

That was because he was still alive. He died five years ago, and I am now writing a monograph about him. I think Saul Lieberman was perhaps the greatest talmudist of all, after the Gaon of Vilna. I will also tell the story of our seventeen-year-long friendship, a deep and

genuine one that went well beyond the usual relationship between teacher and disciple. And I will discuss his
methodology: how he taught, how he wrote. In my view
we can no longer read the Talmud without referring to
and consulting his books.

And Shushani?

He was an extraordinary personality. I met him in
France after the war. He had a deep influence on me.

Wasn't he a little mad?

As mad as can be. He frightened me, but I liked him
a lot, and admired him too. It's curious, because Levinas
and I were his disciples at the same time, yet neither of
us knew anything about the other. Shushani would
sometimes spend days and nights at my place. His last
letter was addressed to me. After his death in Mon-
tevideo, his disciples sent me his documents and
manuscripts. I have a whole history on Shushani. He
was a brilliant and demanding teacher, but somewhat
destructive.

*The first verse of Isaiah, chapter 57, has been interpreted in
contrary ways. The text reads: "The Just perish, but no one
takes it to heart; devout men are swept away, with no one giving it a thought." The end of the Hebrew verse is:* ki mipnai-
hara'a naiaisaph ha-tzadik. *Does this mean that the Just die
before the onset of evil, or on the contrary that they are its first
victims?*

There are several possible readings. I rather lean toward the second one: that they are the first to go, the first
to be swept away in the whirlwind. We saw this during
the Hurban. Children (who by definition are among the
tzadikim, the Just, because they are pure and innocent),

old people, the insane, the sick, the weak—they are always the first victims.

Do your share this thought of Mauriac: "I believe that no suffering is lost, that every tear, every drop of blood, counts."

Sometimes. It depends on the mood I'm in. There are times when I tell myself: yes, all suffering will count, and since God exists, nothing can be lost. According to the ethic of our Fathers, an open book lies before Him in which He records everything; therefore nothing is lost. But there are also times when I look at all the tears, all the pain and suffering and misery, and I ask myself: what sort of book does He have? It must be as large as the world, perhaps even larger still. As infinite as He Himself.

Could you explain the connection between joy and despair in Hasidism? Does joy lie within despair?

There is no lack of despair among Hasidic teachers. They know that it exists. You would have to be thick-headed or insensitive not to know it. The important question is: what do we do about despair? We cannot turn our backs on it, so we must confront it and go forward. But the great genius of the Hasidim was that they found a joy within despair. Indeed, this is the purest joy of all, and the most noble.

Do you mean joy in spite of despair?

In spite of and within despair, for this joy does not deny despair. It is too powerful to be denied. But despite despair, within despair itself, there is a sort of space in which joy is both possible and necessary. Possible because necessary! That is Hasidic joy.

Do you go along with Manès Sperber when he writes that the Warsaw ghetto insurrection was aroused not by hope but by despair, because it was hope that led the Jews to the gas chambers?

I like Sperber very much; he is a close friend. What he says is true, but so is its opposite. With the proviso, as I said before, that when it comes to the Shoah, we cannot generalize. It is true that hope cost many lives, because if the Jews of the ghettos had had less of it, they would have risen up earlier and would have fled in great numbers. In that sense, hope worked against us. But it is too sweeping to say that all the combatants rose up only because they despaired. They still had hope. What did they hope for? First of all to save the honor of the Jews. That was primordial: to save the honor and glory of the Jewish people. To glorify honor implies hope, the hope for a time when honor will be acknowledged and accepted. They also hoped to teach the Germans a lesson. Finally, they hoped that some among them might yet be saved. In other words, despite everything, they still hoped.

Third Day

Speech is exiled even as the words leave our mouths.

Why is it that the new-born infant, cast from its mother's womb, emits a cry of pain? Doubtless because a cry of life is itself an exile's cry.

Exile—absence—is our sole interlocutor. It alone we write.

Edmond Jabes
Le Livre des Marges

The Song of Exile

Philippe de Saint-Cheron: *If someone had told you, before 1944, that a Jewish state would be rebuilt in your lifetime but that you would not live in it, would you have believed it?*

Elie Wiesel: No, and when President Itzhak Navon presented me with the Shazar Prize, I told him so in almost exactly those words: "If, when I was a child, someone had predicted that the State of Israel would someday exist, I would not have believed it. But if I had been told not only that the State of Israel would exist, but also that I would not be living in it, I would have believed that even less."

Where has your sense of exile been strongest? In Sighet, the small town of your childhood, in France after the war, or in the United States, where you have lived for nearly thirty years?

The sense of exile was strongest during the war. War itself is total and ultimate exile. In wartime creation is exiled, and so is law, which ceases to exist and is replaced by different laws. Life itself is exiled, because death surrounds it, and speech is exiled, because it is stifled.

And if war is exile, our war—the war against the Jews—was the ultimate exile, because there was a process of reduction. The country became a city, the city a street, the street a house, the house a shelter, the shelter a train, and then nothing—smoke. That is exile.

Do you still feel exiled even in peacetime?

Of course. For Jews, at least, the feeling is still present, but different. Exile in peacetime makes us feel uncomfortable. It's a kind of reminder: Watch out, you will not be here long; you come from somewhere else, and someday you will be going somewhere else. But that is the creative side of exile.

All your work—from Night, Paroles d'étranger, Signes d'exode, *to your latest novel,* Twilight—*is deeply marked by exile. Is it exile from the dead or exile from a land? And if the latter, is the land Sighet or Israel?*

It depends on the theme. When I deal with Jerusalem, then exile is everything that is not Jerusalem. When I deal with exile, then everything that lies within exile is in exile. There is the exile of exile.

But what does exile really mean to you? Is it a metaphysical or a geographical absence?

Both. I experience it metaphysically because a writer probably experiences certain things more intensely and a Jewish writer even more so.

Our entire epoch seems marked by both exile and madness, as though man has a choice between exile and dementia. Is the act of writing a greater victory over exile or over madness?

For a writer, writing is a victory when it justifies itself, when it recounts what the writer seeks to recount. But when a cleavage arises between the writer and his writing, then writing becomes his defeat. It all depends on the meaning of what is written, on the fire that inspires it and on the fire it inspires. If writing is a victory—and sometimes it is—then the triumph is over forgetfulness and the evil that ravages so many countries and peoples. As I see it, to triumph over forgetfulness is itself an achievement. But writing cannot triumph over exile. In our tradition we are taught that exile will persist even with the advent of the Messiah. When the Messiah comes, he will read the book written by the prophet Elias, but this is a book of suffering, of suffering gathered from all over the world. If the Messiah remembers our suffering, then the memory of exile will remain even after his coming. Writing therefore does not eliminate exile. It persists, but hopefully as redemption and not as destruction. Exile that symbolizes suffering can degrade man, but it can also raise him higher. It is the writer's task to make sure that his writing helps to raise man higher and not to degrade him.

In the Jewish tradition, there is frequent mention of the exile of shekhina *and the exile of speech. Do these two terms mean the same thing?*

The word "exile," a mystical term, is the same. *Shekhina* in exile, *shekhina* exiled from itself. God abandons Himself. This is a very beautiful, poignant, and tragic theme: *shekhina* foresakes God so as to return to us.

Isn't this somewhat similar to the cabalists' theme of tsimtsum: *the contraction of God?*

No, *tsimtsum* is something else. Certainly, it is also part of mysticism, but it is not the same theme as the exile of *shekhina*. God recoils from Himself to create the world: that is *tsimtsum*. The exile of *shekhina* is a different concept. Once the world has been created, and men are suffering, God wants to suffer with us. That is why He allows His *shekhina* to leave Him, so as to suffer in His name, with Him and His creatures. The "exile of the word"—*galut hadibur*—is also part of mysticism, as is the existence of exile. On the divine and universal scale, the cosmic scale, everything is in exile. Including speech. Which means that it no longer conveys the meaning it hopes to communicate.

When we say that shekhina, *the presence of God among us, is in exile, are we to understand that God suffers with man, that He feels sympathy?*

Yes, He suffers with and sympathizes with the suffering of human beings.

With the release of Shcharansky, Sakharov, Elena Bonner, Joseph Begun, and some Christians, have the doors of exile really begun to open in the Soviet Union?

Every time a prison gate is opened, it opens not just for one prisoner but for the whole human race. Unfortunately, prisons open rarely and in too few countries. There are still thousands of prisoners of all kinds in so many countries!

Is there any hope that the Jews of the USSR, the Refuseniks, will be allowed to emigrate?

I have been working on their behalf for twenty-two years now, and so have others throughout the world. If Gorbachev's philosophy is real, if he truly wants to open his country up to freedom, liberalization, and liberation, and if this is also to apply to the Jews, then that would be fine. But I am not so sure. I think we have to wait and see. When I was in the USSR in October 1986, there were still fifteen prisoners of Zion; today, eighteen months later, there is no longer a single one. The Soviets have made some changes. During my trip, after the Nobel Prize ceremony, I participated in the campaign for Yossif Begun. They released him. Several other Refuseniks and dissidents have also been given permission to leave the Soviet Union as a result of our efforts. The signs are good. But don't forget that there are three million Jews in Russia. What frightens me is that the Soviets have passed a law stating that only those who have parents or children, or brothers and sisters, already outside will be allowed to leave the Soviet Union. Most of the people who want to leave do fall into that category. But what about the others? In my view, if we accept this Kremlin decision without protest, then the already serious situation of the other Jews will be threatened.

Isn't the fact that there is now a certain degree of freedom of speech—Sakharov can appear on television, for example—an important event for the Soviet Union?

When I was there, I predicted that this would happen. It is almost as if they were following my advice. I told one of Gorbachev's close advisers that I wanted to meet Sakharov. Day after day, three times a day, I would tell him, "I want to see Sakharov." It was obvious that this made him very unhappy, even more unhappy than when I brought up the situation of the Russian Jews. Finally someone asked me, "Why do you keep asking to see Sakharov? Don't you know that he's in exile?" "Look," I answered, "this is stupid from your own point of view. After all, he holds the only Nobel Peace Prize you have. He has a Nobel Peace Prize and I have a Nobel Peace Prize. Don't you think it's only natural that I would want to meet him?"

"It doesn't make sense, even from your own point of view," I said. "Think about Solzhenitsyn! When he was in the Soviet Union, he was a source of problems and tension for you. Now he's in America, and he's no longer a danger to you. Sakharov, in exile in Gorky, irritates you. Then bring him home; let him come back to his friends!" That's what I said during the press conferences. I also said, in my Oslo speech: "I consider the forced isolation of Andrei Sakharov just as revolting as the imprisonment of Yossif Begun and the exile of Ida Nudel."

In the end they brought Sakharov back, and today he is playing by Gorbachev's rules.

Do you think he's doing that consciously, or has he fallen into Gorbachev's "trap"?

Sakharov is a very noble humanist figure. I admire and respect him. He is a man who has paid his dues, and he deserves the respect of the entire world. He believes that Gorbachev offers a possibility of hope, and he is therefore going along with him. And indeed, compared to his predecessors, Gorbachev does represent a possible opening.

In your book Souls on Fire *you wrote: "Forgetfulness lies at the root of exile, just as remembrance lies at the root of deliverance." When you say "at the root," do you mean as cause or as effect?*

The phrase is not mine, but the Besht's, or rather, it is a paraphrase of the Besht. [The Besht is the title of the Baal Shem Tov, or Master of the Good Name, who founded Hasidism in Poland in the eighteenth century.] In my view, forgetfulness is both the cause and the effect of exile.

In the same book you write that Rabbi Israel of Rizhin said that the sins of Israel were not the cause of exile, but that exile came before our sins.

Yes, Rabbi Israel of Rizhin was trying to defend Israel. And he was not alone in this. There were many Hasidic teachers who said: it is Your fault if the Jews are sinners.

They are sinners because life in exile is hard, so hard that they have no choice. They therefore sin because they have no choice. Bring them back, and You will see that they will be just and good children!

Personally, are you for a very orthodox Judaism — strict observance, if I may use the term — or do you think Judaism should be more open to modernity?

For me a Jew is a Jew. I oppose all varieties of fanaticism, and I am not God's policeman. It is not for me to say who is a good Jew and who is a bad Jew.

Are you still a Hasid?

Of course. I define myself as a Hasidic Jew, which means that I belong to the Hasidic tradition. But I regard the entire Jewish community as my community.

Is the congregation you usually attend Hasidic?

The temple I go to is a personal matter. Naturally I try to lead a somewhat more exigent life, because I have the right and duty to demand everything of myself, but I must also be as tolerant of others as possible.

*　　*　　*

Had I asked an indiscreet question? The answer would suggest that I had. But on reflection, it was not so much the question as the answer that was indiscreet, for Elie Wiesel does not like to talk about personal matters. A few months later I happened to be rereading One Generation After, *a book he wrote eighteen years ago, in 1970. And I was surprised to find in it exactly the answer I would have wished for. The text may be out of date, since Elie Wiesel no longer lives at the same address, but it remains as moving as ever:*

"Very close to my Manhattan apartment, there is a modest Hasidic house of prayer—a shtibel *—that reminds me of those I knew in my childhood. Except that in this one the services are held in the basement. The worshippers are mostly refugees. Former residents of Warsaw and its surroundings, they bear traces of its long hours of agony. All have known the reality of concentration camps. None speaks of it except during the holidays. And as I listen, I understand what Rebbe Nahman of Bratzlav meant when he expressed the wish that his tales be transformed into prayers."*

This brief text introduces a chapter that Elie Wiesel entitled *"Excerpts From a Diary." Every one of its fifteen pages tears at the heart, recounting memories of some of the great holidays of the Jewish year, and of one Hasidic celebration in particular. Beyond the memories, there is an ineffable nostalgia for a world—and a joy—gone by, one the Hasidim revive in their little Manhattan chapel, as they do in other places as well.*

Many of Elie Wiesel's books—such as The Gates of the Forest, Paroles d'étranger, *and of course* Souls on Fire—*feature Hasidic holidays. His Judaism is closely tied to Hasidism, and his emotions, memory, and nostalgia are bound up with the Hasidism of his childhood and the people he met then.*

One night in December 1975, during a speech in New York, Elie Wiesel spoke of the memory of a Hasid he encountered in the kingdom of night: "I remember that nameless and faceless master whose words we received as offerings we were duty bound to share and pass on. He spoke to us of the Torah and the Talmud, and I learned more from him than from all my other masters. Every word he spoke was ringed by a circle of fire, just like those spoken by Jonathan ben Uzziel in the Talmud."

*   *   *

Philippe de Saint-Cheron: *Do you regard the atheism and agnosticism of our epoch as dangerous for the future of humanity?*

Elie Wiesel: That is difficult to assess. As a religious man, I would say yes, but when I consider the evil that religions have done in the name of their faith!

But the contrary is also true: in all the countries in which God and religion are banished, man is eventually reduced to the status of a thing.

That's true. I am not a defender of atheism or agnosticism.

But these are related questions.

In the end it comes down to fanaticism. A fanatical atheist is dangerous, and so is a fanatical believer. Sometimes even more so.

Are you frightened by the rise of Islamic fundamentalism throughout the world, particularly in the Iran-Iraq war and in Lebanon, which is threatened by so many varieties of fanaticism?

It is a dangerous and disturbing phenomenon. Dangerous for the entire world. Fanaticism allows and justifies everything. Imagine if Khomeini had atomic weapons! There is no doubt that he would have used them against Iraq, and once atomic Death is unleashed, no one will be able to rein it in. But that is not the only danger of fanaticism. The fundamentalism of others responds and corresponds to Islamic fundamentalism. We are seeing a disturbing rise of fundamentalism and fanaticism throughout the world, among Christians — Protestants and Catholics alike — and even among Jews, both in Israel and here in Brooklyn. And that troubles me. Fortunately, they are a small minority.

Are you pleased that the European Parliament has officially recognized the genocide against the Armenians? And are you troubled that the resolution passed by only 68 to 60, with 42 abstentions?

Yes, that is troubling. Neutrality always troubles me.

But isn't this official recognition a victory for the Armenians nevertheless?

I am against Armenian terrorism and violence, but I think that the Armenians have the right to know, the right to remember, and the right to make sure that the entire world remembers. Long ago I proposed that a colloquium be held between Armenians and Turks to discuss this tragedy, but the Turks refused. I still believe that such a meeting ought to be held, because it is futile to try to forget.

But isn't the attitude of the Turkish state similar to that taken by German courts when they sentenced several Nazi criminals to very brief prison terms?

I would not make that comparison. Nothing can be compared to that Event. What we have here are two instances of injustice, and I speak out against both. But I would not like to compare the criminals or the attitude taken to the criminals. The fact that the world has forgotten the Armenian tragedy is very serious, and the reason I wrote a preface to Franz Werfel's book on the Armenian massacre, *Les 40 jours de Musa Dagh*, was that I wanted it to be remembered. If I can help, I will.

It is significant that the author of that book is an Austrian Jew.

Yes. He was moved by their tragedy. Jews are moved by the tragedies of others.

Pierre Emmanuel wrote somewhere: "Faith cannot be reduced to the things of this world, for in that case there would be nothing beyond man, and if there is nothing beyond him, then man is nothing." Do you share that view?

There is much that I share with Pierre Emmanuel. But here he is raising the question of God, of God beyond man, and God is not beyond man. I like to think that God is at man's side and not above him.

Do you mean that there is no transcendence, or rather that transcendence is nothing?

Even immanence can be nothing. Without transcendence, immanence is meaningless, but without immanence, transcendence has no meaning either.

It seems to me that what Pierre Emmanuel was trying to say is that faith—in this instance Christian faith—is nothing in the absence of hope of life after death.

I don't know. What happens after . . . I would not like to venture into that terrain.

How do you explain the fact that of the fourteen million Jews in the world today, barely half are religious, whether orthodox or liberal? Is this part of a more general phenomenon of loss of divine meaning and faith, or is it a consequence of emancipation, extreme assimilation, or even the Shoah?

I don't know. Statistics is not my field. How do we decide if someone is religious or not? By whether he goes to synagogue or is a member of a temple? Who can say that one person is religious and another is not? It is more difficult to observe a non-religious person, because a religious one goes to synagogue. But how do we decide about the others? It's difficult. I don't like to classify people like that. Only God knows, and He has not yet decided to make His voice heard.

Isn't the Return of a part of the people of Israel to Zion the great miracle of the past two thousand years of Jewish history? And isn't it also the first step toward the fulfillment of messianic promises?

A miracle, yes. Or at least the great event, certainly the greatest positive event, of the past two millennia. As for whether it constitutes the first step toward the fulfillment of messianic promises, some Hasidic schools say so. In Israel, in fact, all the Jewish congregations say the same prayer for the State of Israel, one that is also part of the liturgy in the Diaspora. It contains the phrase *raichit tzmi'hat geoulatainu*, which means "the beginning of the redemptive promise," the promise of Redemption.

How is it that even after the reduction of six million human beings to dust and ashes, the people of Israel were still able to recover so strongly in the Diaspora?

This is one of the mysteries of the Jewish people, and it is not a new one either. Look at what happened during the Crusades, or the pogroms. The books of Jewish history tell us that the enemy attacks, uproots, and massacres our community with iron and fire.

But afterwards, we know not how, a new community rises out of the ashes and begins to live again. Where does this community find the courage to survive, to organize itself anew, and to keep alive while awaiting the next massacre? This has been going on for two thousand

years now, and I think that this mystery is part and parcel of the other.

*But something entirely new has been added with the crea-
tion of the State of Israel. This time the Jews have come together not simply to await the next massacre but to defend themselves, and sometimes, as in Maalot, to respond. And that, of
course, raises the question of the cycle of violence, which also
involves the self-defense so indispensable if Israel is to live and
not merely to survive.*

This is a constant danger. I often think of Israel with
anxiety and anguish, but Israel also offers us many reasons for hope. This country, which is only forty years old
and has gone through so many ups and downs, so many
trials and tribulations, has nevertheless managed to re-
tain its human identity. If I compare Israel to the idea Israel ought to have of itself, then naturally there are problems and unresolved conflicts. But if I compare Israel to
any other country—to France with Algeria and Indochi-
na or to America with Vietnam, not to mention the Soviet Union—Israel always emerges as more human than
other peoples, who have done or would have done
worse in similar circumstances.

*Jacques Ellul has said that the world would not survive Is-
rael's destruction.*

I fear that this is true. The destruction of Israel or of
any other people would entail the destruction of the
world.

*Why is it that whenever the Torah speaks of the fear we must
have of the Lord, verses always follow about orphans, widows,
foreigners, the deaf, the blind? Is fear of the Lord most essentially fear for others?*

God is not in me alone; God is in others.

Fear of God — irat hashem — *is fear* for *Him and* for *others?*

That is the essence of my Hasidic interpretation of the phrase. Fear of God — *irat shamaim* — is not simply fear of God but also fear *for* God. In other words, fear for God the creator and fear of God in His creatures.

In Signes d'exode *you wrote, "That is what we learned from Auschwitz: it is impossible to live and die solely under a question mark." We need answers!*

Yes, but there are none.

Song

Philippe de Saint-Cheron*: I have had the pleasure of hearing you sing* Ani Maamin, *a song that was part of your childhood and youth. Song has an irreplaceable liturgical value in our tradition. Is it specifically linked to exile or has it acquired a different significance since exile?*

Elie Wiesel: Don't forget that song played an important role at the Temple of Jerusalem too. The tribe of Levi were the singers and composers, and I am a Levite, a descendant of that tribe. Some varieties of Christian liturgical music, the Gregorian chant in particular, originated in the liturgy of the Temple. But in exile the Temple exists only in our dreams, prayers, and aspirations, which is why the song for the Temple becomes more fervent then.

Because it is sung in times of ordeal and against suffering?

Yes, against suffering. A song that expresses suffering is a voice raised against it.

It was your grandfather Dodye Feig who taught you to sing. It was also he who taught you the Hasidic tradition.

Yes, he was the one, along with my mother, who taught me the beauty of song. Everyone in our home sang Hasidic songs—even my father, who considered himself emancipated.

The word chant *figures in the title of two of your books,* Le chant des morts *and* Ani Maamin, un chant perdu et retrouvé. *Have you ever experienced one of those moments when words and language are paralyzed and man's only choice is to sing or keep silent?*

Yes, but singing is not the only option. I would like my writing to become a song, and I mean that physically. In fact, I need music around me as I write, and I mouth the words as I write them.

When you returned to Auschwitz, was that one of the moments when words and language were reduced to silence?

Several years ago, we went to Auschwitz and Birkenau on Tisha b'Ab.

In Birkenau there is an incomparably dense and unique silence. I remember feeling that it must have been as silent as that when God gave the Torah on Mount Sinai. It is as if you are standing at an invisible altar on which a third of our people were sacrificed. After a very long silence, I heard the words Shma Israel, first as a murmur, then as a shout. Words that have been the final cry of so many Jewish martyrs.

Do you believe that there is greater power in song than in words?

Undoubtedly a more mysterious power, since everyone can respond in his own way, with his own imagination. Rebbe Nahman of Bratzlav used to say that every person, every human being, has his own song, and so does every object. Every tree has its song, every leaf and blade of grass. The whole world is an immense song, a

vibration that flows from being to being and object to object. Without this song, it is not the world that would be
mute, but we ourselves: we would not hear, we would
be deaf and dumb. It is through song that we rise toward
heaven.

*Has it ever occurred to you, while listening to a Bach cantata
or a Beethoven symphony, that music reaches further than
words?*

Often. I am envious whenever I hear a beautiful piece
of music. I say to myself, If only I could have written
that!

The rabbi of Lubavich, the Baal Hatania, as we call
him, said: "When we face a question that has no answer,
the only response is to sing." Song becomes an answer
to unresolved questions, but song itself is also a
question.

Isn't music the art that brings us closest to God?

We musn't exaggerate or generalize. What about
someone who doesn't like music or song, who is insensitive to it? Or what about a deaf man or woman? Is a human being who is born deaf unable to come closer to
God? It is well that other paths exist. For such a woman
or man, then, the road to God goes not through music,
or perhaps through a different music. For a painter, the
road is through painting, for a dreamer through the
dream. And for a writer or poet, through writing. Still,
I love music.

*But doesn't this mysterious power of music lie in the fact
that literature is made of words, and paintings of colors and images which, however transformed, in some sense already exist
in nature? Do we speak through singing?*

But this power exists in poetry too, and also in silence.

Do you agree with Cioran's statement: "Only since Beethoven has music been addressed to men; before that, it conversed only with God."

Cioran is a great writer. But what about Bach, Schütz, or Pergolesi? Or the Baroque or Renaissance composers? What about the great choral works, the masses. Granted, that was religious music, but at bottom these compositions were also addressed to people. The composers may have been thinking of God as they wrote, but surely they also had in mind all the people who would hear the music in church, and later in concerts.

In The Gates of the Forest *the rabbi says to Gregor: "There is joy as well as fury in the Hasid's dancing. It's his way of proclaiming, 'You don't want me to dance; too bad, I'll dance anyhow. You've taken away every reason for singing, but I shall sing. I shall sing of the deceit that walks by day and the truth that walks by night, yes, and of the silence of dusk as well.' "*
Where have you found this sense of joy in the dance and song of Hasidism, apart from among the survivors, of course?

Most of all in the Soviet Union, but also in Jerusalem. On the day Jerusalem was liberated, during the Six Day War, the entire country—men, women, and children— danced and sang in the streets of the city, in tears. The atmosphere was almost messianic.

But wasn't there also a kind of revolt in this song?

Yes, it was a revolt.

Is it through song that the believer rises highest toward the Blessed Holy One?

It is dangerous to toy with restrictions like that, claiming that God listens more to this or that. What do we know of God? Perhaps He likes song. But perhaps not. Maybe one day He will return to Sinai and say to men: Listen, idiots, you're all nuts! You thought you were giving me pleasure, but the truth is that your singing annoys me no end!

Do you recall singing during deportation?

We sang at the beginning, when we first got there. For a few weeks. Then we stopped.

The Talmud contains a sublime phrase about song, spoken by God to His angels as the Red Sea closed back over the Egyptians: Ma'assei yadai tov'im bayam veatem omrim shira!, *"My creatures are drowning and you have the gall to sing!" Are there times when even song is no longer possible?*

The beautiful thing in the Jewish tradition, in ancient Jewish culture, is that there is no song or celebration of war. War is waged when necessary, when there is no choice. But we have no right to glorify it. In all our tradition, where do we find song? After crossing the Red Sea, Moses, along with all the people, sings out of recognition that they have been saved. In the book of Judges there is the song of Deborah after the war with Canaan. But look at the book of Joshua, a violent book full of bloodshed. Here poetry is lacking. It is the least poetic of all the books of Scripture, and I am convinced that there is a reason for this. It is telling us, in effect: Listen, when you fight, when you have to kill or be killed, you don't sing. You have no right to sing when people around you are being cut down, for to sing then, or to write poetry, would be to glorify war, and war must not be glorified, for its countenance is ugly and hateful.

Only the victims can be glorified?

And how do we glorify the victims? By loving them.

Isn't every human being's first prayer a cry, a plaint, rather than a eulogy or song?

When a baby comes out of its mother, it cries. It cries when it discovers the world, and rightly so. But the first morning prayer of the Jews is a thanksgiving. "I thank Thee for having awakened me." It reminds me of the Hasidic saying: "The true cry is the one that goes unuttered," the cry suppressed.

You have written: "Who is a Jew? The man or woman whose song cannot be stilled by any enemy."

It is the song of the Jews that sustains them, but here I mean song as a symbol of the soul, the memory, of the Jews. Song is also the sap that rises in this memory.

But your statement seems to go further, since it could be understood to mean that any man or woman "whose song cannot be stilled by the enemy" is Jewish.

True, my vocabulary and terminology are Jewish, but the phrase ought not to be interpreted that way. To say that the Cambodians suddenly become Jews because they are suffering would be condescending to say the least. I love them because they are, and because they suffer. It is as if they too were to say, "He whose song cannot be stilled is Cambodian."

In The Town Beyond the Wall *you write: "Man may not have the last word, but he has the last cry. That moment marks the birth of art." Is that how you experience your act of creation?*

The instant that precedes creation is personal. For me it is always a time of anxiety and joy. Anxious joy and joyful anxiety. Sometimes I tell myself that it is silly to write, that there are easier occupations. But I could not live without writing any more than I could live without studying and teaching. A mystery? The fact is that for an artist, for any writer or creator, there is nothing so mysterious as the moment when something within him or her begins to take shape, to be revealed, whether in painting, music, or literature. If the creator knew what that something was, if he was aware of the mystery, then he could no longer create.

That's why so many creators are depressives, or even go insane.

Because they don't know. We have no right to know, it would be dangerous to know. It comes from the deepest part of our being. It is buried somewhere within us.

The power to recreate worlds—to give new life to human beings, to make the imaginary real—is a tremendous power, one that transcends us, is it not?

I have always felt that way. I feel my own limits, I sense the obstacles. But what choice do I have? How could I stop? We have no right to stop. So I go on. I do the best I can. As Samuel Beckett said, "en désespoir de cause." Since we cannot do otherwise, we create.

Is artistic creation—which Pierre Emmanuel called "procreation" in contradistinction to God's Creation—a continuation of the Almighty's work?

Since we cannot create, we recreate vanished worlds and perished beings.

Fourth Day

Death, Life

Philippe de Saint-Cheron: *Do you consider death the su-preme injustice, the supreme exile?*

Elie Wiesel: Death is absolute. Like God, like life. What else can we say? What is death? How can we imagine it before it comes? Of course it is an injustice. In Jewish religious life, it is the ultimate negation, injustice par excellence; it is ugliness, impurity. Some mystics maintain that death is the first offense, because it represents a kind of blasphemy, a stain on creation. That is why death must not be exalted, which explains why there is no philosophy of death or literature of death in the Jewish tradition. Unlike the Egyptians, we have no Book of the Dead.

That would also explain why Jewish messianism is more temporal than metatemporal.

Exactly. But Jewish messianism is so complex. What is the Messiah? A man, a movement, a time, an era? In fact, we speak of the messianic era and messianic time much more than of the Messiah.

This terrestrial aspiration for the Messiah suggests a power greater than death, an irreducible protest against it. We do not accept death.

And a protest against history too, against the Hegelianism of history seen as advancing toward its conclusion, its end.

What do you think of Malraux's claim that "death is the irrefutable proof of the absurdity of life," and that "nothing—no divine thought, no future recompense—can justify the end of a human existence"?

Quite true. I could find equivalent words in the Talmud: whoever kills a human being, it is as though he has destroyed the world; whoever saves a man, it is as though he has saved the world. Judaism rejects death completely. We recognize that it is inevitable, but we do not summon it. On the contrary, for us life and the living are pure; death and the dead are impure.

There are those who think of death as an expiation. Is that a genuinely Jewish thought?

In general, it is true that some Masters accept the idea that death is expiation for sin. But others say that if it were that simple, there would be no hell and no idea of hell.

This came up earlier, when we were talking about Céline and Brasillach, but I would like to ask it more directly. Are you opposed to the death penalty?

Yes, as a general rule I am opposed to it, but I could imagine cases in which I would have to be more circumspect, in particular where the murder of children or the hijacking of commercial airliners is concerned. Then I would be more severe. In the Eichmann case, I agreed with the court's sentence, which I considered just. In general, I am indeed against the death penalty, particularly because of the spectacle that is created around it. I find that obscene.

What do you think of the notion of a statute of limitations on crimes against humanity? To have a twenty-year statute of limitations for crimes like that—and perhaps for others too, in particular when children are the victims—would seem to amount to offering a pardon, de facto if not de jure.

Wouldn't this be tantamount to wiping these crimes out, as if time were a natural means of expiation? Does the Jewish tradition have a concept of statute of limitations?

It does have a concept of so-called cities of refuge, but these are only for involuntary killers. In cases of deliberate murder, there is no statute of limitations; the perpetrators must be tried whenever they are caught. If a defendant is found guilty, he is sentenced to death. Except that in the Jewish tradition the task of witnesses is difficult. Our legal tradition is centered on testimony much more than on appeals to judges. The witnesses are decisive. If two witnesses say, "We saw this man commit an intentional crime," then he must be sentenced to death. But the task of the witnesses is so arduous that it is almost impossible to obtain a guilty verdict.

But there is a talmudic adage that a sanhedrin, *a tribunal, that issues two death sentences would be branded murderous.*

Indeed, death sentences are very rare in the Talmud.

So the death penalty exists in Jewish law, but no judge in Israel would apply it with impunity?

It exists as a deterrent, but is not meant to be applied.

What does the last judgment represent for you? At bottom, who is judging whom?

Suppose it was the dead who judged us? Their verdict would be severe. Perhaps they are already judging us. At the Barbie trial, I said something that some people found upsetting: "If I am testifying here today, it is not for the dead, because I am convinced that one day the dead themselves will speak, and on that day the earth will tremble."

They will speak, I don't know how, but the dead will find their intermediaries, their interlocutors. Perhaps they will speak through us. But one day they will speak.

Is it conceivable that the dead will seek vengeance?

This goes beyond vengeance. For the dead there is no such thing as vengeance, but there is something else: justice. And the justice of the dead is not the justice of the living.

Is the fight against death a hopeless battle, or should we see life's struggle against death as proof of man's greatness, and perhaps of his victory over fate?

Both views are correct. We must struggle against death, and as long as we do, we are immortal. Every man is immortal so long as he lives, so long as he fights, walks, writes, and creates, all the while knowing that he is mortal. We are made of flesh and bone, blood and dust. But when it sprouts and grows, a shoot of dust is immortal.

Some human acts testify to life and to victory over the forces of evil and death. Courage, for example, or artistic creation, or love. . . .

Creation survives. Man dies, but other men live. That is why both theses are valid: man has every reason in the world to despair and every reason in the world not to.

Once again, it is a Pascalian choice, and it is up to us to opt for one road or the other.

How do you understand the incomparable mystery of fatherhood, apart from the obvious joy of being a father? Did you see this as a kind of response to absurdity, an answer to ashes and dust and death?

To have a child is probably the most agonizing possible response for a man, but also the most powerful!

In A Jew Today *you wrote: "Why did the survivors have children? By what right did they give us life?" Ten years later, do you have an answer to that question?*

It still seems valid to me today, yet the survivors did marry (sometimes even remarry). They built homes, had children. Despite everything, they proved that they had faith in the future, faith in man and in man's humanity.

They bore witness to hope!

"Hope" is perhaps too grand a word. But certainly to faith, albeit a faith limited to the moment, a hope limited to their circumstances.

The Jewish tradition, in its very essence, faces toward to the future. Psalm 128, which we recite every night before going to bed, says: ourai vanim levanekha shalom al Israel, *"May you see your children's children. Peace be upon Israel."*

But the opposite is true as well: we also have a tradition of ancestors. Children must accept the faith of their fathers in a chain that goes back to Abraham. Every Jew is a link in that chain.

*Balzac's Father Goriot said, "When I became a father, I un-
derstood God." Are you struck by that phrase?*

It would be a little difficult for me to say that I have understood God. I can see how Balzac, who had a febrile
literary imagination, might have written such a phrase.
But I am only his reader.

*But isn't the gift of paternity, like that of maternity, the only
thing God allows human beings to share with Him?*

Balzac may have had in mind the Christian concept of
the Son of Man. Don't forget that he was educated under
Christian influence and that his writings reflect Christianity, even if unconsciously.

*If human beings could be shown in advance what their lives
would be like and were then offered the choice of being born or
not, would you have opted for life despite everything?*

The Talmud says that it is better not to be born than
to be born. It is more comfortable not to live, but since
we have been born, we must live. I was born, therefore
I study. We are not asked whether we want to be born,
any more than we are asked whether we want to die.
Another passage of the Talmud says: "We are born by
constraint, and by constraint will we die."

*"And by constraint will we be judged," Rabbi Eleazar Haka-
par teaches in the* Pirqai Avot, *the treatise of fathers.*

Exactly.

*One of the first questions I asked you was whether you felt
that the compassion and impossibility of vengeance that are so
prominent in your work constituted a kind of victory over the
hell you suffered. "The word 'victory' is too strong," you an-*

swered. But do you ever think of your own personal achievement as a remarkable revenge against your fate, as a victory for the forces of life and good over those of death and absolute Evil?

"Victory" is a word that says nothing to me. I would rather call it a response, or an attitude, to hatred. I have never felt hatred. I have never allowed this tragedy to be reduced to mere hatred. Whom would I hate, even if I wanted to?

There were so many murderers, and so many accomplices.

Like many others, I have simply tried to make something of my suffering, to make something of our past. Sometimes I think I have succeeded, sometimes that I have failed. But in either case, to my mind this is the sole legitimate response. Other people have had other ideas, such as going into business, for example, or even getting rich, while others have gone into politics. But I have taken my own road.

Would you say that the will to live is transcendent in an ordeal as horrible as the one you suffered—one which has since taken other forms, such as the Gulag or Pol Pot?

I don't know. Why generalize? For some people it was, for others it was not. Some say that they tried to survive so as to bear witness, others because God wanted them to live. A collective disaster has such sweeping scope that every individual must be allowed to react individually. Every person's identity and response must be respected.

Would you say that placing fear of others' deaths above fear of one's own is an ethical utopia, a reality, or a moral duty?

There is no such rule, because man does not have the right to sacrifice himself for another. We talked about this earlier. *Kayekha kodmin*, your life does not belong to you, your life comes before that of others. Yet whenever someone sacrifices his life for another, we hold him up as an example. But the word "other" in your question is too vague. Exactly who is this other? If it is my son, then certainly I fear for my son more than I fear for myself. I would like to help him to avoid all ordeals. Where fear is concerned, I start with the person closest to me, which is only human; otherwise he would not be close to me.

But don't you feel that there is something exemplary, some-thing admirable, in fearing for someone who is not close to you but is close to someone else—the sort of sentiment embodied in people like Albert Schweitzer and Janusz Korczak in the past or Dom Helder Camara and Mother Teresa today? Isn't there a supreme disinterested charity that makes one fear for others more than for oneself?

Let's be realistic. How many Janusz Korczaks and Mother Teresas are there in the world? When God hand-ed down the Ten Commandments on Mount Sinai, he was addressing not only the Just, but all men, and not only the children of Israel, educated people, or saints. Yet few listen.

You often say that you do not understand atheism, but don't you think that revolt within faith and atheism both represent ways of defining one's relation to God? The ultimate protest against Evil and absurd suffering, so to speak.

Naturally, atheism is the most current form of protest against God. The atheist says, If evil exists, how can God exist?

But doesn't atheism nevertheless attest to an idea of God?

Doesn't the atheist have a particularly clear vision of what he thinks God ought to be if there was one?

As you see it, yes, but not as the atheist sees it, for it is you who say this, not the atheist. Atheism's attestation to or confirmation of God is therefore valid for you, but not for the atheist. Otherwise he would not be an atheist.

Perhaps we ought to distinguish between two kinds of atheist: the indifferent atheist for whom the question does not even arise, and the atheist who is motivated by a fierce hatred of everything to do with God and religion. If the latter sort of atheist is motivated by this kind of hatred, isn't it because he wants to believe in an all-powerful God?

You may feel that way when you look at him and listen to him, but an atheist who believes in God is suspect. In any event, it is all too easy for believers to say, "Look, friend, since you say you don't believe in God, that means God exists." If the atheist says that he does not believe, let us at least respect his conscience.

I would like to digress here, though to an essential topic. Does being a Jew mean simply believing in a particular religion, Judaism, or does it mean belonging to a people, Israel, which is unique in the world, a people more metaphysical than geographical?

It means belonging to a culture, a tradition, a religion, and above all to a collective memory. To be a Jew is to participate in the collective destiny of Israel.

When you talk about the people of Israel, the Jewish people, does the term have a primarily metaphysical or geographical and racial significance?

Not a racial significance. It is the anti-Semites who speak of a Jewish race, not us. We speak of metaphysical, ethnic, geographical, and historical consciousness.

François Mitterrand recently gave a speech at the Sorbonne in which he said that the French were also a little Italian, a little German, and a little Spanish. Then he added: and also a little Jewish and a little Arab. Is this what you mean?

François Mitterrand was trying to be generous, saying that every people, every country, is actually a mixture of various peoples.

But many, especially in France, would not agree with that. "How can you be French and also belong to the Jewish people?" they would say.

There are many things about the Jews that people do not understand. So what?

But some Jews say this too.

That's true. They probably don't understand either.

Do you agree with Claude Vigée that Israel is "the only possible response of the Jewish people today"?

Certainly it is one of the most exalting responses. But I don't think it's the only one.

After this digression on the Jewish people and Israel, let me return to the question of death. Do you believe that death has the last word, or do you think that memory is somehow stronger than death?

Memory is stronger, but not for the dead themselves. Only for the living and for children yet unborn.

What is it in man that is strong enough to look death in the eye when the time comes? In raising this question, I have in mind particularly the fighters of the Warsaw ghetto, or the Jews of Masada, who preferred to kill themselves rather than fall into the hands of the Romans, or Rabbi Akiba and Rabbi Hanina ben Teradion, who died martyrs of the faith.

It's faith.

Not sacrifice?

First of all faith. Sacrifice comes later, because only then does one know what the sacrifice is for. Faith is therefore the foundation, while sacrifice follows, because without faith sacrifice would not be possible.

At the same time, sacrifice transcends faith, or in any case sustains it.

And contrariwise: faith sustains sacrifice. Faith therefore comes first, but faith can take various forms: faith in God, in man, in art. . . .

In Twilight *you wrote: "The victim's only superiority over his torturer is that the latter is never satisfied." I don't understand what that means.*

The torturer is an unfortunate man indeed. Even more unfortunate than his victim. He fears his victim's freedom, his victim's truth. That is why he is a torturer. And he fears his own solitude, for the torturer is in fact more alone than his victim. The study of the encounter between victim and torturer raises agonizing questions, but the victim surely triumphs in the end, because even if he dies — most often in atrocious suffering — for the torturer nothing is solved. He will only seek another victim.

Then even in death — in fact, through his own death — the victim wins victory over the executioner. It still seems hard to understand.

I am not saying that the victim is any more fortunate. On the contrary, he is extremely unfortunate, for he is suffering and is going to die. He suffers, and the torturer has a need to see him suffer. But the torturer — absurdly evil and cruel — still remains unsatisfied, because his sadistic needs are never sated. He's an imbecile, worse than a wild beast that has to stalk prey today and yet again tomorrow.

Because the wild animal hunts only to eat, which is hardly the torturer's intent.

Yes, wild animals kill to feed themselves, but in a certain sense, torturers also feed on their victims. But the sadistic needs persist, and the torturers know this full well. They can never stop. Machiavelli wrote that political murder is stupid, because no dictator, no potentate, has ever managed to kill his successor.

Of all your books, Dawn — *even more than* The Fifth Son — *seems to be the one in which the main character is not a victim. He is a survivor of the death Camps who has to kill a hostage British officer to avenge a member of a Zionist organization executed by the English.*

No. He is still a victim, perhaps one who finds himself constrained to kill, but he is not an avenger. He is compelled to use a power that he does not want but that has been forced upon him. This book about violence is an indictment of violence. It is meant to show quite starkly that there are certain things that a victim must not do. The key to the novel, in fact, comes when the hero, Elisha, says, "It's done. I've killed Elisha." In other words, Elisha has not simply killed the other man: by killing the other man, he has also killed himself.

In a certain sense, however, the pioneers of the Jewish state did achieve victory over their enemies.

In 1959, when I wrote *Dawn*, I saw it as an imaginary novel, for I had not lived in Palestine at the time the action was set. I knew nothing of the reality. Sometime later, I met an Israeli who had been an important leader of the underground resistance during the British occupation of Palestine. "You're completely crazy if you think it really happened the way you wrote it," he told me. Yet for me that is how it happened. There must have been constant anguish, constant questioning. Even if it did not happen the way I wrote it, I still think this must have been how things were: you have to think a long time before killing someone, and it must also be agonizing not to kill in the end.

When you were a young Hasid in the village of Sighet in the Carpathians, were you already conscious of the tragic sense of life caused by exile and death?

Of course. We were in exile, and in exile you are aware of that. Except that we knew how to deal with that feeling, and even how to turn it into joy and faith through prayer, and into friendship through dreams and ambitions both mystical and human. But the feeling was there despite everything.

We cannot live in exile without that feeling. This comes back to your title: Evil and Exile. There is evil in exile. How can evil be exiled? That is the question. A big question. Our Masters said that after the advent of the Messiah, evil would be exiled, punished, and reduced to nothingness.

And so would death. At the end of time, our exile in death will be supplanted by the exile of death and thus by the death of exile.

Yes, death too will be exiled and reduced to nothingness. Death itself will be annihilated; it will be the death of death.

How did you rediscover life after your release from Buchenwald? Do you remember your first thoughts when you were free again?

I do. My first desire, my first wish, my first project, was to pray. To say *kaddish: yitgadal vyitkadash chemeh rabba* (may His name be magnified and sanctified!). To say *kaddish* was my first thought as a free man. It was my first impulse, and those were my first words.

To celebrate God on behalf of the dead, on emerging from the abyss!

To glorify God, and also to accept Him. Revolt came later. And that is how it should be: first we accept, then we question.

For the survivor, aren't the mysteries of survival and death radically and absolutely opposed to one another?

That's all right. As I told you before, I'm not afraid of contradictions.

Shma Israel

Philippe de Saint-Cheron: *Can we not suggest a new reading of the words Shma Israel, "Hear, O Israel"? Suppose we eliminate the vocative and read the noun "Israel" as the direct object of the verb. The phrase — "Hear Israel" — would then be directed to the Christians and the Nations: Hear what Israel has to tell you! Hear what God has to tell you through His people, Israel!*

Elie Wiesel: That is a beautiful, correct interpretation, but I think that we must start with the *pshat*, the evident meaning. The primary meaning of Shma Israel is the one given in the Torah: "Hear, O Israel, the Lord thy God, the Lord is One." It is Israel that must listen, Israel that is being summoned, called upon to heed the Lord. Later, of course, we can try anything. The meaning and structure of the phrase can be altered and extrapolated. Every new meaning is then added to the previous ones.

But if the Nations really listened to Israel . . .

If the world heeded the Jewish experience and Jewish history, I think it would be a better place.

I would like to ask a more personal question about this. You are a man who has been heard, who has been heeded. Yet recently you said, "My life has been a series of failures." Aren't you overlooking not only your work and the moral authority

*you have won (which earned you the Nobel Prize), but also
your son and the many other people who have been helped by
your words and your example, people who love and admire
you?*

A series of failures in the practical sense. We have
tried to do various things, to undertake certain actions,
but with no success. We have tried, for example, to eliminate anti-Semitism, but it still exists. We have tried to
struggle against hatred, but it is still rampant. We have
tried to banish war, but still it rages on. That was what
I meant.

*But if even just a few people heed the word of peace, isn't that
enough to make it meaningful?*

A single person is enough.

*How do you interpret this passage of the Talmud: "Since the
destruction of the Temple, divine inspiration has been withdrawn from the prophets and bestowed upon children and
madmen"?*

The destruction of the Temple was an outrage, a religious upheaval that resulted in terrible collective suffering for the entire Jewish people. This event was therefore the *hurban*, destroying not only the Temple and
Jerusalem, but also the Jewish nation as a whole.
Prophecy itself consequently had to be withdrawn, out
of respect for that suffering. Now, what is the meaning
of this passage of the Talmud? It is a sort of parable, and
a very striking one. Does it mean that every child is a
prophet and that every madman possesses the gift of
prophecy?

*You mean that children and madmen are endowed with a
kind of intuition that we lack?*

No, not exactly. Perhaps we might say that prophecy, as divine inspiration, is important for children, who have not yet begun to learn, who have not yet drunk at the well of knowledge. They do what they do on impulse, by intuition and instinct. Like madmen, in a sense.

The Babylonian Talmud reports that after the destruction of the Temple, Joshua ben Hattaniah said: "Do not mourn, for we cannot. . . . But neither can we mourn too much." Could this statement be applied to the Shoah as well?

Definitely. Some people have had the strength and courage to live in that world alone, a world of suffering and of memory of suffering. Personally, I have not done so. Of the thirty books I have written, only five or six deal directly with this question. The others exalt life and the Bible, Hasidism and the Talmud, the Midrash and mysticism, Jerusalem and the Jews of the USSR. Like Joshua ben Hattaniah, I feel that we must not live in constant mourning, in the memory of suffering.

But is this a victory over yourself or not?

No, no. I study. It is study that has saved me.

Precisely for that reason study is the foundation of all religious life in Judaism, for it gives rise to prayer and action.

As we say in the morning prayer, *Talmud Torah keneged kulam.* The study of the Torah is worth all other virtues and all merits.

Which means not only that study leads to prayer, but also, strictly speaking, that it is itself . . .

. . . a prayer.

Many of our contemporaries believe that there has been too much talk of the death camps and the Shoah over the past forty years. What is your reaction?

Those who say such things have never really read anything at all about the Event. They have not even begun to read the documents or to listen to the testimony or even to see the films. For them it is an excuse not to read, not to listen, and not to watch. Those who have already read do not say such things. On the contrary, they want to read more. Really, there is no point in arguing with such people.

Is it a refusal to look truth in the face?

It is a deliberate refusal, lacking in generosity. All I can say to these people is that I have encountered this phenomenon of rejection of truth before in my life. When an individual represses certain things, they reassert themselves later with extreme violence. If humanity today tried to banish all this suffering, all this agony, all this death and all the dead, it would all come back someday, rising up against the entire world with destructive violence. That is exactly why we must remember; you might call it therapeutic. Except that remembrance is not merely therapeutic. It also involves something higher— something more urgent, solemn, and majestic.

But in the meantime, are these kinds of statements of any real importance?

Yes. They teach us that we must work harder, that we must write, speak, and teach more and more. Then perhaps such statements will someday be impossible.

Isn't anyone who dares to reject and falsify this truth fundamentally evil and insensitive?

Some people are insensitive, obtuse, and indifferent.

Isn't there something blasphemous about the ignoble lies of the "revisionists" in particular?

To blaspheme is an act, a commitment, whereas insensitivity is nothing. I often say that there is nothing worse than indifference.

At bottom, the Jewish contribution to humanity, the messianism bequeathed by the prophets of Israel, is hope against all odds, is it not?

Messianism is hope that persists *despite* evil. This consciousness can also be seen in Jewish resistance throughout history, through the centuries of exile in the Diaspora. We must continue to hope despite evil—not merely to heal it, but despite it, despite despair and the sadness that lingers in despair's wake. We must hope, and we must live. That is why we must preserve our own identity, while also respecting the identity of others.

Do you believe that love is stronger than death or merely equally as strong?

It would be more human, more humble, to say—as the *Shir ha-shirim*, the Song of Songs, does—that love is *as* strong as death. Love is as strong as death. That is a striking image. But to say that anything is stronger than death. . . . Life itself is not stronger than death. A single rifle is enough to make all the world's wisdom vanish.

Do you think that evil will outlive man in the end?

No, personally I think and hope that man's thirst for good is stronger than his thirst for evil, and also stronger than evil itself.

Fifth Day

Anti-Zionism is a miraculous find, a providen-
tial windfall that brings together the anti-
imperialist left and the anti-Semitic right; anti-
Zionism makes it possible to be democratically
anti-Semitic.

Vladimir Yankelovich
Pardonner?

From Anti-Semitism to Anti-Zionism

December 8, 1987

Philippe de Saint-Cheron: *You are particularly concerned by the meeting between Gorbachev and President Reagan on nuclear arms reduction. Don't you think that it is dangerous for the European countries to be completely excluded from this meeting, which is of prime concern to them?*

Elie Wiesel: I understand that the Europeans are worried, and I can see why they might be suspicious. It is true that the two "great powers" are getting together to decide the fate of Europe. As it happens, though, I am no expert on strategic questions, however much I am concerned about the threat to humanity they represent. Nor am I a political scientist. My main concern and interest is human rights. I believe that everything must be viewed from the vantage point of human rights, on an individual scale. And here I am worried. Five days before his arrival in Washington, Mr. Gorbachev made a statement that seems alarming. He has shown that he is much too hard—even inflexible—on the question of human rights and especially on the question of Jewish emigration. This is very serious. Everything hinges on the issue of trust. If we can trust him, then it will be all right, but can we trust him? Tentatively, I would say Yes. He has, after all, done some admirable things.

Things no one in the Soviet Union had done in a long time.

He has released people from prisons and camps; he has unlocked doors. For that I am grateful. I applaud what he has accomplished in this domain. But it is not enough. Today, for the first time in a long while, there is an openly anti-Semitic organization in Soviet Russia. People tell me that it is a small group, but it is a very active one, some of whose members met with Mr. Gromyko several months ago. Its existence and activities are known to one and all. A number of Soviet officials told me, "We can't put them in prison anymore, you know, because this is not the same old regime." Well, in that case I would like to bring back the old regime for a little while, if only to deal with them, to put them in prison. It is unthinkable for there to be anti-Semites in Soviet Russia, where everything is official. Moreover, Gorbachev said some things on American television that I cannot understand. He spoke of a "brain drain." What does that mean? Can a brain be imprisoned? In the end, I am still suspicious of Gorbachev.

About a year ago you said something on French television that made a big impression on me: that you could not trust a man who spoke of nuclear arms reduction while letting hundreds of thousands of people languish in camps and psychiatric hospitals.

For me human beings are the barometer. How can I expect a man to have compassion for humanity if he has none for the individual who lives alongside him?

Are there any "prisoners of Zion" in the USSR today?

Happily, no. They have all been released. Some are already in Israel, while others are visiting here in the United States. I also intervened on behalf of some cancer patients who have been allowed to join their families abroad for medical care. The balance-sheet on all these coordinated efforts is therefore rather positive in several respects. That's why I am pained when I see Gorbachev allowing himself to be manipulated – unless it is he himself who is doing the manipulating, in which case he is far more Mephistophelian than I feared.

Last Sunday – the day before his arrival here – we organized a large demonstration in Washington. Two hundred thousand people participated. On that same day Gorbachev had a group of Refuseniks dispersed in Moscow, and an American commentator was arrested. What is the meaning of that?

I would like to ask you something about an event that made quite a stir in France last September: the National Front leader's characterization of the gas chambers as a "mere detail." In a democracy, can any action be taken against such political provocateurs?

I made a statement about this on Human Rights Day, when René Cassin's remains were transferred to the Pantheon. I said then that this person was odious. A "mere detail"! What is a "mere detail"? No human being is a "detail." When he calls millions of human beings a "detail," it shows what he really thinks of humanity in general and the Jewish people in particular. I cannot understand how a man like him has the position he does in France, and I hope that by revealing himself as he did, he alienated those French people who unfortunately still believed in him and his "mission."

But at the same time, isn't the existence of people like him a sign of democracy?

The strength of democracy is precisely that once such people are unmasked, once they are seen for what they are, they are rejected. He must therefore be rejected.

Do you think that democratic countries ought to pass a law like the "Auschwitz is a lie" statute enacted by the Bundestag in 1985, which allows the prosecution of people who deny the reality of the Camps?

Personally, I would favor that, but I am not a lawyer, and lawyers tell me that there is a constitutional problem with this law. Freedom of expression cannot be limited. But something ought to be done, at least for some time, because I can well imagine the damage such statements do, the pain they cause the survivors. This law ought to be adopted, if only to protect the sensibilities and the mental and physical health of the survivors and their children. How? The question is beyond me; it is a legal problem.

*   *   *

Do you remember the first time you arrived in Israel?

I came to Israel by ship in 1949. I was a journalist at the time. The tension I felt went beyond mere excitement. I stayed up all night so I could stand on the deck at dawn and see Israel rise up before me. I was silent. The ship was filled with emigrés, and I remember that the "Olim" had been singing during the voyage, but that morning they stopped. There was a deep and reverent silence on the deck, and when we finally sailed into Haifa, everyone felt like applauding, but no one did. The applause was internalized; emotions ran high. I discovered Israel little by little. First Haifa, then Tel Aviv, and finally Jerusalem. At that time, the old city and the Temple wall did not yet belong to us. Jersualem was reunified only in 1967. So I sought out every nook and cranny from which you could see the old city. I climbed a tower and spent silent hours gazing into the distance. I was sad, but my mind was at ease. I watched soldiers of the Arab Legion patrolling in the old city, but the sight of them did not depress me, for it was but an aspect of exile. Jerusalem was still in exile, and since the city had been in exile for as long as I could remember, it seemed natural. It was only in '67 that we realized how much finally lay before us, how much our Jerusalem, Jewish Jerusalem, meant to us.

Do you feel that in some sense Israel is still in exile today— exiled from peace?

We have no right to say that. Heavenly Jerusalem may be in exile, since it still awaits redemption, but terrestrial Jerusalem will remain in Israel, as Israel is in Israel. Some Jews may be outside Israel, but Jerusalem will remain the capital and the heart of the people and of the country.

Do you believe that a rapprochement between Arabs and Jews is possible?

I believe it because I have to believe it, otherwise there would be no hope.

Isn't there an understanding between Muslims and Jews in Jerusalem itself, in the old city?

I cannot tell you that. I don't know, because on my trips I don't stay long enough to get a really clear idea of what's going on in the city. I definitely believe that relations exist on the individual level, but individuals cease to be individuals once politics comes into play.

If you lived in Israel, would you contest some of the government's policies and actions?

Yes, of course. I am sure that in Israel I would participate in the daily life of the country, including social and
cultural life.

Yankelovich once went so far as to protest against Israel,
during the war in Lebanon in 1982. But he regretted it and
even wept about it.

I was disappointed to read about that in the papers.
I admired Yankelovich, and I was sorry to see him
demonstrating outside the Israeli Embassy. A Jew's
place is inside, not outside.

How did you learn of the events in Sabra and Chatila?

I found out about it on Rosh Hashanah. Despite all the
media attention, deep down I didn't believe it. I thought
it was impossible that some Jews—for we now know that
only a few Jews were on the scene and involved—would
permit such acts of barbarism. How could Jews in Israel
have been complicit in such a massacre, I asked myself.
I couldn't believe it. I had appeared on the French television station Antenne 2 *before* Sabra and Chatila, during
the siege of Beirut. I was on my way back from Israel
then, and I remember saying that the French press was
not dealing honestly with Israel. I begged my col-
leagues, my former collaborators, to be more understanding, more loyal. I told them that they were completely ignoring the sadness in Israel, Israel's sadness.
  As I was leaving the studio, a journalist I knew well
said to me: "You have no right to say that today. The
only thing you can do today is condemn Israel." It was
a very difficult time.

* * *

At that moment, a friend of Elie Wiesel's telephoned from Israel, and he went to answer. I was impressed by the completely natural facility with which Elie Wiesel moved back and forth between French and Hebrew, English and Yiddish, the four languages he lives with, shifting through memory and history. "You see, Michael," he said when he came back, "we were talking about Israel, and that was Israel on the line. When Israel calls, you have to respond. And not with an answering machine."

As a Jew, I love Israel, but sometimes I wonder whether the prophets, if they returned today, wouldn't rail against the Israeli leaders, summoning them to a greater ethic.

I cannot give you an answer. As I said, I am in the Diaspora, and I have no right to interpret or extrapolate the thought or will of the prophets. If I was in Israel, I would say certain things, but not from outside.

Is Israel in solidarity with the great causes affecting the world's least favored countries, such as famine relief or the fate of the Boat People?

Israel was actually the first country to welcome Boat People, back in Begin's day, before France and before the United States. As for famine and refugees, I can tell you that wherever I go, I encounter Israelis. When I was at the Cambodian-Thai border, I found Israeli doctors in all the camps. Israel has shown impressive generosity toward all those who suffer, who need medical care. Yes, when I go to countries in difficulty, I often encounter Israelis who have come to help, to care for people, and also to bear witness.

Israel and Elie Wiesel's Sadness

Early 1988 was marked by sadness and anxiety. Passions were unleashed by events in Israel and the occupied territories. On several occasions Elie Wiesel had to take a public stand on this political and historical reality. His words were distorted and attacked by the press and by certain Palestinians. In February he spent several days in Paris, giving his annual address to the Rashi Center on Rabbi Meir and his wife, Brouria, two controversial figures of the Talmud. Three-quarters of the way into his speech, he stopped to share his sadness with us. At that moment, everyone felt that the essence of the message he sought to convey that evening lay in this digression from the formal subject of his address. Here is what he said:

"This time, I must tell you, I bear within me a kind of anguish and sadness. I sense a climate so very hostile to Israel. I do not mean — and I have never said — that everything done by men and women in Israel must always be approved and justified. But I have also said — and I repeat — that it is important and necessary for us, the sons and daughters of a traumatized generation, to love Israel. In certain circles in France today, to say that one loves Israel is to expose oneself to stupid and insulting criticism and accusations. It is as if we could not love the Jews without at the same time hating their neighbors. As if we were not pained to see Palestinian children struck. Yes, we are pained, every Jew feels pain. But we are also

144

pained because we know that those who must fight in Israel have no choice.

"I must tell you that I know of no solution. I hope that there is one.

"Do you think that there is a single Israeli soldier who enjoys what he's doing? I am ready to swear on the Torah that not a single soldier is acting with joy or pleasure. But that is forgotten. They impugn our motives, because we love Israel and because I say, 'I love Israel.'

"I love Israel even in sadness, and at this moment there is a sadness in Israel.

"I love Israel even in its hour of trial, and Israel is going through a grave and painful trial."

Elie Wiesel's feelings about the serious crisis Israel is now going through have never been what some people have suggested they are. The most important thing is that the truth be heard. Yet it is clear how difficult this is when every word spoken by a man like Elie Wiesel is automatically interpreted, twisted, and falsified even before it is pronounced. Objectivity and impartiality are sorely lacking. But it is nevertheless surprising to note that while the Palestinians all accused Elie Wiesel of justifying the Israeli repression—which, of course, he has never done—not a single one sought a dialogue with him.

Philippe de Saint-Cheron: *Do you agree with Franz Rosenzweig's comment in* The Star of Redemption: *"It is society itself that defines to what extent the assimilation of the Jews can be tolerated"?*

Elie Wiesel: I think that the Jews themselves and not the societies in which they live ought to determine those limits. The choice is ours. We are entitled to two privileges: deciding who is a Jew and deciding who our enemies are. Some of our enemies like to claim that they are actually our best friends.

Well, these people can shout all they want, but the

Jews must have the courage to say: No, you are not our friends, you are our enemies.

When a French, American, or Russian Jew says that he belongs to the Jewish people, isn't that a gift to anti-Semites, who can then claim that it proves that they are not French, American, or Russian, but Jewish?

That is a classic accusation, but it has never bothered me. Personally, I consider myself both Jewish and American, yet I love Israel with all my heart and I write in French. I am close to all these countries. It is the Jew in me who is American, the Jew in me who loves France, and the Jew in me who loves Israel with all his heart and soul. Perhaps there was a time when we had to make these geographical choices, but today geography has disappeared.

You believe, then, that affirming your Jewishness and remaining deeply attached to your own tradition makes you even more French or American.

Absolutely. As Judge Brandeis said back in 1930, right here in the United States: "It is because I am a good Jew that I can be a good American."

A very curious phenomenon is the recrudescence of anti-Semitism in Japan in the past few years, recently aggravated by the rise of serious economic and financial problems. Last year the infamous Protocols of the Elders of Zion was issued by a Japanese publisher, and several dozen anti-Semitic books have appeared in recent years. Isn't this somewhat surprising, given that there are no Jews in the country?

This is one of the reasons why I went to Japan last June. I visited three cities and spoke to various audiences. "This is really insane," I told the Japanese.

"There are no Jews in your country, yet you are still anti-Semitic. How can you fuel and justify this anti-Semitism?" And indeed, there are a total of about five hundred Jews in Japan, perhaps one of whom is a Japanese citizen: the rest are foreigners. Five hundred Jews in a country of one hundred million inhabitants! That is why I warned them: "Listen! Anti-Semitism is not your concern. It is a European disease, and better left where it is, in Europe. Be happy that you are not part of that atmosphere!" Well, of course they replied that it wasn't true, that there was only an anti-Semitic literature, but no anti-Semites. And I answered, "But the fact remains that a million copies of a book by a certain Uno were sold—a million copies!—and that means something, whatever you say." In his book, Mr. Uno repeats all the archetypical anti-Semitic arguments, to the point that wherever I spoke, I always had to begin with a joke:

"Believe it or not, Rockefeller is not my cousin, and Wall Street is not under my control." In fact, some Japanese think that the Rockefellers are Jews, that the Jews are responsible for the rise or fall of the dollar or the yen, that the Jews are everywhere, that they control the whole economy. Anyway, I went to Japan to try to initiate a dialogue with them. I also met a Japanese Christian, the author of a best-selling book on the Jews. "Here in Japan there is interest in the Jews," this man told me. "What does it mean that my book was such a success, and that anti-Semitic books also sell so well? Only that the Japanese are interested in the Jewish people. It does not mean that they are anti-Semitic." But I was not convinced. I remain uneasy. Indeed, isn't it troubling that anti-Semitic books have appeared—there are already about thirty of them—and have achieved such popularity?

Paradoxically, the imperial family is said to be very philo-Semitic.

Yes, especially the brother, who is said to have wanted to convert.

Before 1940, Bernanos was an anti-Semite, whereas after that date he became so philo-Semitic as to write: "It is an honor to remain Jewish and to have Jewish children, enough of them that all the pogroms will fail to annihilate what God has ordered preserved." What is your impression of him?

I very much admire Bernanos the writer. But that is partly because of his later positions. His initial anti-Semitism disturbed me, as did his friendship with Drumont, of course. But for a "rightist" author to have had the courage to take the position he did during the war in Spain was to exhibit great perspicacity. It was clear that Bernanos was going to come toward us. His discovery of what the Jews represent is testimony to his openness and generosity. In France, perhaps in all of Europe, it is almost impossible to find a writer who did not go through an anti-Semitic period, at least before the war. It is not his fault, moreover, because we musn't forget the political and literary atmosphere that prevailed at the time. That is why I bear no grudge against Bernanos, who had the courage to oppose fascism, to condemn anti-Semitism, and to say what he did about the beauty and honor of being Jewish.

And about the duty of remaining Jewish.

Yes, and about the duty of remaining Jewish.

But there are two French writers who never went through an anti-Semitic period: Camus and Malraux.

That's true, but neither Camus nor Malraux came from the "right." However hard you look, you won't find a "rightist" author who did not go through an anti-Semitic period. Without realizing it.

Do you think that John Paul II's trip to the United States in September 1987 was positive for Judeo-Christian relations, particularly his encounter with the Jewish community? Wasn't it in Miami that he acknowledged for the first time—officially, at least—that "Israel's existence is fundamental for the Jewish people"?

I cannot discuss this, because I was supposed to meet the pope in Rome on August 24, a week before the rabbis, but for very personal reasons I decided to postpone that meeting. It is still in the cards, however, and will probably take place in 1988. I prefer not to talk about it until then.

You were supposed to meet him in the Vatican?

Yes, I was invited officially. Not for an audience, but for a private conversation. Yet I had certainly criticized him. I was probably his most sustained critic in America. Because of the Waldheim affair, of course, which shocked me deeply, but most of all—and we have already talked about this—because of the mass he celebrated for all the victims in Birkenau, a place where, as everyone knows, the immense majority of the victims were Jewish. I criticized him quite openly, but several cardinals called me and suggested, in his name I imagine, that we meet. I agreed, but then postponed the meeting. We will reschedule it.

What was your reaction to the announcement that the Vatican is preparing a document on the Shoah, more than forty years after?

I cannot discuss it without having read it, and it has not even been written yet. When it is written, I will read it, and I hope that it will contain the whole truth, including the truth about Pius XII. It was not particularly diplomatic of John Paul II to praise Pius XII during his meeting with the rabbis and Jewish leaders in Miami. I tell you frankly that I found it somewhat bizarre and surprising that he felt it opportune to do so.

As for the document, I think it would be irresponsible to try to comment on a text that I have not read and that has not even been written.

Still, whenever it occurs, your meeting with John Paul II will be an important date in Church relations with the Jews. You will be the first Jewish Nobel Peace Prize winner to meet John Paul II.

I don't know; in any event it's possible.

Sixth Day

Mystery and the Ineffable

New York, Wednesday, December 9, 1987

Philippe de Saint-Cheron: *In Monsignor Lustiger's latest book,* Le choix de Dieu, *he is asked a question about the Shoah by Jean-Louis Missaka: "Wouldn't you say that God abandoned men?" Monsignor Lustiger answers: "No. The pain is so unendurable that I can bear it only if I see in it the mystery and compassion of the suffering Messiah."*
What is your view of his response?

Elie Wiesel: My view is that there is no response. There is simply no response to the Shoah. Auschwitz has no answer. Any response, whether human or theological, is a bad one.

But doesn't the attempt to find an answer testify to Christian good conscience to some degree?

Not as I see it. I will admit that if the Messiah were to come tomorrow, then men would cease to suffer. Then—and only then—we might perhaps conclude that the advent of the Messiah was a response to the great suffering that had gone before. But not even the Messiah could change the fact that six million Jews, a million and a half of them children, were murdered. So even the coming of the Messiah would not necessarily offer an answer to that enormous and unjustifiable suffering. But to call the suffering Messiah a response today! No, in my view Auschwitz remains a question without an answer.

Then Buber's notion of the eclipse of God and your own questioning are really the only things we can dare to say in face of that abyss?

Exactly. All we can do is ask questions and wonder.

In Christianity, Jesus proclaims that he will die for men. Is the idea of a Messiah who takes the sins of men upon himself, expiates them, and dies for their salvation really a Jewish idea? And conversely, can the Jewish people be seen as having "died for God" in the Shoah, as "having taken upon themselves the unimaginable guilt of God's indifference, absence, or impotence," as George Steiner has written?

No, that is not a Jewish idea. Suffering for others, even for God, is not a Jewish notion. This kind of suffering is not part of our tradition. The martyrs' *kidush-hashem* [literally: sanctification of the Name (of God)], far from accusing God, glorified Him.

Yet so much of the suffering in our history seems — or at least might seem — to have occurred in God's cause, or for God.

Yes, there is much suffering, but we have not spawned a theology of suffering. The very formulation of your question implies a theology of suffering, and to make a theology out of suffering borders on justifying it, something we have no right to do. Even to say that we suffer for God would be to claim a justification and religious significance for the suffering men have inflicted upon us.

You mean that it is actually much simpler . . .

It is much simpler because we do not know the answer. But the moment we turn suffering into an answer, we thereby justify that suffering by ascribing a meaning to it. And that would be to betray both the response and the suffering.

As a question, then, . . .

For me the only possible path remains harsh, rigorous, and lucid questioning.

But doesn't Israel, by which I mean the Jewish people, have the countenance of a suffering Messiah?

Well of course we can find similar analogies in the Midrash, but our tradition is not so quick to accept this comparison. In general, our sages would not like us to be messiahs.

In Claude Lazmann's film Shoah, *the question, "Why" is asked only once. Standing in front of a church in Chelmno—on the day of the celebration of the birth of Mary!—one of the Poles answers by supposedly quoting a martyred rabbi to the effect that if the Jews were murdered, it was because they killed Jesus. What do you believe the murderers were trying to eradicate by exterminating us?*

Memory. It was essentially a war against memory.

And against God, no?

That is not what they said. What they said, first of all, was that they wanted a world without Jews, a world without Jewish memory. They were killing the Jews in order to kill their memory. I hope that the Christians who saw and heard that Pole's awful comment will understand that he was lying. It is absolutely unthinkable that any rabbi in Poland or anywhere else could have said that we were killed because we denied and killed Jesus.

But there is also Hitler's comment: "The Jews invented conscience."

It is quoted frequently.

Then what the Nazis wanted to annihilate was Jewish memory, and beyond that, Jewish conscience.

There is no memory without conscience, just as there is no conscience without memory. But the prime target of their hatred was memory. They were trying to annihilate the memory of Israel.

Now let me change the subject completely. I would like to know whether you believe that the mystery of life prevails over the mystery of death?

Both are absolute; how can they be compared? One is as poignant as the other. The mystery of good is as great as the mystery of evil, and the mystery of life is as great as the mystery of death. But they correspond to two different kinds of dread: dread of life and dread of death. They cannot be compared: they simply are.

Since man began to think—in other words, since he became aware that he would die and that human life is but a fleeting succession of happiness, separation, and suffering—haven't we been haunted by the mystery of why it is that man has not only accepted life, but has also agreed to give life? How has he managed to live a life marked so inexorably by the dread of death?

This remains a complete mystery.

Isn't the mystery of Israel's survival in some sense similar to this mystery common to all human beings?

Yes, but on another level.

In your view, what is the first question, the one that determines all others?

For me the "first question" depends on many things: the moment, the day, my mood, the situation in which I find myself. But most often, it is the first question asked in the Bible: "Where art thou?" In other words, Where am I? God asks Adam, *Ayaikah?*, "Where art thou?" and this, I think, is the primordial question. Where are you in life? At each tragedy, each situation, we ask ourselves, What is my role in this? Where is my place— whether in God's grand design or in the mean designs of men? What is my responsibility to my child, to the dead, to the living? I try to weave a sort of thread tying me to all these men and women.

In the Midrash man is given this advice: "Know whence you come, whither you are going, and before whom you will account for your life." In fact, that is the Bible's message. But after death, in the other world, the *olam haba*, the first question asked of the dead is: Were you honest in your dealings? That is the very first question we will be asked when we stand before the celestial tribunal.

This text teaches us, once again, that human relations have primacy over all others. The second question is: Did you await the coming of the Messiah?

In Twilight *you write that the first question the angel asked the dead man was: What is thy name?*

Because at that point his soul was still in the grave. But

the first question before the celestial tribunal will be: Have you been honest in your dealings with others?

The Hebrew words ani, *"I," and* ayin, *"nothingness," are written with the same three letters—aleph, yod, nun—and therefore have the same numerical value. Does the twofold equality of the letters and numerical values of these words signify a deeper relationship?*

Of course, there is nothingness in man, but there is also man in nothingness. This is a dangerous game, Michael, but an interesting and amusing one too.

Stunning and incredible correspondences sometimes crop up.

Images. When I was young, I too liked to play with gematria: the numerical value of words. Less so now. I used to think that the Cabala was gematria above all else, but now I know that the Cabala is other things as well.

Havel havalim akol havel. *"Vanity of vanities, all is vanity." Thus begins the Book of Kohailet, Ecclesiastes. And in the same spirit, our morning prayer,* Ribon kol ha-olamim, *asks the believer:* mah ana'hnu, meh 'hayenu, meh 'hasdenu, mah tsidkainu, mah yeshuatainu, mah ko'hainu, mah g'vuratainu?, *"What are we, what is our life, what are our charity, our virtue, our salvation, our power, our strength?" Do all these questions put to us by the authors of these inspired texts mean that life is not worth the effort of living it?*

This corresponds most of all to a particular state of mind. I am convinced that there comes a time when every person feels that life is not worth living. Prayer must reflect our whole struggle, our entire life and all our inner personality, and these texts represent one particular state of human awareness. The prayer itself then helps

to make us aware of our anguish, and the moment we
say "anguish," the anguish is eased.

Do you believe that anguish is fundamental in man?

Certainly. Life, after all, is but a corridor between one
world of darkness and another—or perhaps it is one of
light, but nevertheless unknown. It is therefore only natural that life should arouse fear and trembling. That is
why we accept anguish in Jewish tradition.

*The whole Torah, the whole Bible, teaches us that human
beings have not just one chance, but several.*

This is in contrast to Greek mythology. Indeed,
throughout antiquity, whenever any man had anything
to do with a god, that was the end for him. Men could
never win against the gods. How can victory be won
against a god? But in the Jewish tradition there is *teshuva*,
or repentance. Everything is tied to *teshuva*. Man always
has a chance to return, to save himself. And *teshuva* can
be performed an indeterminate number of times,
provided that one does not say to oneself, I repent so as
to sin anew. In that case *teshuva* is not valid. Every
repentance must be sincere and complete. Even if there
is backsliding later, at the time of repentance man must
be sincere.

*But isn't there also a concern to love the Torah as much as
one loves God?*

For us *ahavat Torah*, love of the Torah, is important indeed. Moreover, the Torah is presented to us as a person. The Jew has a personal attitude toward the Torah,
an intimate love for it. In the Talmud this bond is so extreme that God, we are told, consulted the Torah before
creating Adam, and sometimes He talks to the Torah,

which answers Him. The Torah is therefore like a living person, and in that sense we love it as much as we love God.

Is it conceivable for agnostic, or even atheistic, Jews to remain faithful to the Torah?

Faithful to the study of the Torah, I would say. In fact, some agnostic Jews do study the Torah. We used to joke about it: in some countries there are atheist Jews who love the Torah so much that they spend the Sabbath poring over it, puffing on a cigar or cigarette. [Smoking is forbidden on the Sabbath.] To believe or not to believe is one thing, but to study is something else.

Is it not through study that the religious Jew can conquer anguish?

Yes. In fact, it is written in the Talmud that when someone's head is pained—in other words, when he feels anguish—there are several possible solutions: first he looks within himself, then he reflects upon his other occupations, trying to put them in perspective, and finally he studies.

Wasn't it love for and fidelity to the Torah more than confidence in a silent God who seemed to have abandoned them that bound the Jews in the Camps to Judaism?

Here again you are looking for an answer that does not exist. Even in the Camps, there were some who believed, just as there were others who did not believe or who ceased to believe, and others still who continued to practice. Even there I met Jews who refused to eat non-kosher meat; some of them were close to me, like my friend Rabbi Manashe Klein. He himself knew the rabbi of Klausenburg, who never once ate non-kosher meat in the Camps. That was really something! I still remember a childhood friend from Sighet who would always trade meat for potatoes. We have no right to generalize. The subject is too serious, too grave.

Jewish Thought and Commentaries

Philippe de Saint-Cheron: *When you first read Martin Buber's* Gottes Finsternis (The Eclipse of God), *were you surprised that he never explicitly mentioned God's silence during the Hurban?*

Elie Wiesel: Yes, I was. Buber is one of a number of Jewish thinkers who did not take a position on the Hurban in their works. Abraham Yeshua Heschel is another. I didn't know Buber personally, but Heschel was a sort of older brother to me, and I know that he died a thousand deaths at the merest mention of the Hurban. Yet it is virtually absent from his writings. I don't know about Buber. He returned to Germany very soon after the war, to receive the Frankfurt Peace Prize, and he tried to explain himself.

Did your Master Saul Lieberman write anything about the Event? Did you talk about it with him?

He never wrote about the Hurban, but of course we talked about it. I am convinced that many Talmudists think about it and ponder it, but in their own way, through study.

Is there any such thing as Jewish theology? Franz Rosenzweig grasped the very essence of Judaism when he wrote in The Star of Redemption: *"Of God we know nothing."*

He was not the first to say so. Maimonides made the same point. Not being a theologian myself, I find it difficult to judge the matter. But I don't think there is Jewish theology in the same sense as there is Christian theology. We speak of a Jewish tradition, of Jewish thought and a Jewish quest, but not of Jewish theology.

Is it conceivable that there could be Jewish thinkers worthy of the name outside the religious tradition?

Don't forget that there are agnostic Jewish thinkers too. Who am I to deny that they are Jewish? Even if they are agnostic, they have the right to call themselves Jews and Jewish thinkers.

But doesn't the term "Jewish thinker" usually refer, at least implicitly, to religious thought based on the Torah and on the entire tradition?

Yes, but there is non-religious Jewish thought too. A non-religious Jewish thinker possesses other keys and references, and approaches things differently. There have been many Jewish writers, especially in Yiddish, who were not religious. You can't say that they weren't Jews or that they didn't write Jewish works. But they were not necessarily believers, even though they may have referred to the Torah and quoted the Talmud. Their thought was not religious.

Paradoxically, can the works of Marx and Freud be read as eminently Jewish in their essence, insofar as they deal most deeply with what is human in man?

Some have said so, but I am not a specialist in either of them. I only know that some say that this proximity exists.

But Freud did write a book about Moses . . .

Which I did not like at all. It is far from his best work.

*But I'm also thinking of Marx, who wrote that profoundly
Jewish, even biblical, phrase which George Steiner quotes in
his passionate, paradoxical study* La longue vie de la méta-
phore, une approche de la Shoah: *"Marx asks that man
'exchange love for love and justice for justice.' "*

Steiner forgets that Marx was a virulent anti-Semite.
How can we lay claim to Marx? He wrote the worst
pamphlets, of the sort turned out by Goebbels and
Streicher. In the text you're talking about, Steiner also
mentions Karl Kraus, who detested the Jews. Yet he was
a Jew himself.

Like Marx?

Different from Marx, since Kraus, though less pro-
found, was more brilliant. More forceful.

What was Freud's attitude toward the Jews?

Freud made no secret of his Judaism. You cannot compare him to Marx.

*Still, it is curious that Marx, Freud, and Einstein — the
three men who most revolutionized not only the West but the
entire world in the past hundred years, whether for good or
ill — were Jews. And Kafka could be added in the realm of art
and poetry.*

We are the leaven.

*I would like to return to George Steiner's text for a moment.
It seems problematic in more than one respect. For example: "It*

may be that German is the only language in which anything intelligible or responsible can be said about the Shoah."

George Steiner said that last year, at a symposium on the Holocaust held at the University of Haifa. Many Jews from Central Europe, survivors, were in the audience that day, and they were appalled by his words. What about Yiddish, the language of so many of the witnesses? Or Hebrew. But Steiner does not know those languages. How can he sweep away all the most moving testimony? I myself originally wrote *Night* in Yiddish. Furthermore, how can he say that the language of the hangmen is the best one for talking about the Hurban? Some intellectuals don't like survivors; they find them embarrassing. Which is understandable enough. After all, survivors strike fear; they upset things.

Earlier you said that Judaism had no notion of "suffering for," that everyone must bear his own suffering. But aren't there passages of the Torah in which one person shoulders the trials, dangers, or suffering of the people in order to save them? Not only Moses, but Esther too exposed herself to danger to save her people and was ready to die for them. Several weeks ago Emmanuel Levinas showed me a most extraordinary passage of the Shabbat treatise in which Isaac, alone among the patriarchs, takes upon himself the sins of Israel that it might be saved.

There are such images, of course. Esther, however, suffers not *for* others, but *with* them. And Isaac suffers his own ordeal.

The Midrash says somewhere that Adam himself gave up the last seventy years of his life that David might see the light of day.

But he lived nine hundred and thirty years. Which is not bad! We must be clear about this. No concept in the Jewish tradition is so exclusive or dogmatic as to admit of no exceptions. Yes, we find some formulations that point in this direction. A sage once said, "May my death be a source of redemption for others!" In other words: may I suffer that others might be spared suffering. Another Master said, *Tehai mitati kapara lekol beth Israel*: "May my death be a kind of expiation for all the people of Israel." Certain Masters spoke such words just before they died. But this attitude cannot be generalized or turned into a doctrine.

There is nevertheless a very stunning passage, page 60a of the Houlines treatise of the Babylonian Talmud, which recounts a dialogue between the Moon and the Lord, based on Genesis 1:16. After the creation of "two great lights," the biblical text immediately refers to the "greater light" and the "lesser light." The Moon complained: "Lord of the universe, is it possible for two kings to wear the same crown?" And the Lord replied: "Then make yourself smaller!" Then, when He saw that the Moon was not satisfied, He added: "You will offer a sacrificial goat for expiation in honor of the Lord," which the Hakhamim read: "for the Lord."

The question I am raising is whether we can say that whereas Christianity developed the notion of a God who redeems men's sins and dies for them, in Judaism it is incumbent upon man to atone for the Lord.

There are indeed passages in the Talmud that say that the Lord suffers.

But this passage from the Houlines treatise says the opposite: it is not man who has done something wrong and is redeemed by the Lord, but the Lord who has done something wrong, and man must offer a sacrifice of atonement for Him.

The sense of the passage is that God should not have belittled the moon. But the whole beauty of the Talmud is that it may say anything—and indeed does. The inspiration and imagination of the Hakhamim are such that everything is possible, everything is permitted. But I am not sure that Judaism and Christianity necessarily stand opposed on this particular notion. Because God is also present in the opposition. Our lack of knowledge of God is such that God can be in this very lack of knowledge.

I would like you to clarify several verses of the Torah for me. First of all, in chapter 27 of Bereshit [Genesis] there is a verse that seems particularly ambiguous to me. Isaac says to Esau, Veal 'harbekha ti'hiyai, *which is usually translated: "By your sword you shall live." But since the word* al—*spelled* ayin, lamed—*means "on" or "with," shouldn't the traditional meaning be reversed, as it is in the Midrash Rabba, to read: you shall live without—and not with—your sword?*

*   *   *

Elie Wiesel gets up and goes to the shelf behind his desk, where he keeps the essential books: the Torah, the Talmud, and the Midrashim. Before picking up the volume of the Midrash Rabba, he covers his head with the kipa, *as every Jew must do before undertaking a biblical or talmudic reading or study, or before entering a synagogue.*

This is the first time since the start of our encounters that Elie Wiesel has delved into one of those large folio volumes with several styles of Hebrew letters on each page: the fully vowelled text in the center, the commentaries, called Rashi, in small characters at the foot of the page and on either side of the principal text. These books roused me to reverie, for they contain the bottomless wells of Jewish tradition in which Elie Wiesel and Emmanuel Levinas, my other Master, were born. For the past four years, it has been my privilege to listen to Levinas every Sabbath at the Ecole Normale Israëlite Orientale in Paris, where, after the service, he grants us an hour of the light of the Torah, along with his commentary, based on the Rashi and on a page of the Talmud drawn from one of these venerable volumes.

Elie Wiesel has just found the passage I had quoted.

*   *   *

Elie Wiesel: "Thou shalt live with thy sword in its sheath." That is how the Midrash reads it. *Veal 'harbekha,* which must be read: "Sheath thy sword to live." But there is also the interpretation you cited, in which the Hebrew *al* is read as the Aramaic *oul,* which would mean: "Thou shalt live without thy sword." The commentary explains: may thee have thy sword, may thee possess it, but may thee not use it. I had not remembered this text.

Philippe de Saint-Cheron: *Next is a passage of Shemot [Exodus] which the Gospels have made famous by distorting its meaning. In the Gospel of Matthew, Jesus condemns verse 24 of chapter 21 — ain ta'hat ain, "eye for eye," which he interprets as a call for vengeance — as the exact opposite of his doctrine of forgiveness, compassion, and love for one's enemies. Isn't this a serious misinterpretation of the Hebrew verse? Moreover, doesn't the translation falsify the deeper meaning of the three Hebrew words* ain ta'hat ain?

Our interpretation is different. In the rabbinical tradition, in rabbinical law, it is never eye for eye, but the value of an eye for an eye. The issue here has to do with damages and compensation: the value of an eye for an eye.

But isn't it dangerous to allow such a text to be translated that way? Most French Bibles include no annotation of it, and I suppose that the same is probably true of translations in other

*languages. In France even the edition published by the rab-
binate translates it that way without further explanation!*

A note is necessary, even indispensable. In all of Jewish history there has never been a case in which an eye
or a tooth was taken from a person guilty of any crime.
Never.

*And yet the vengeance interpretation seems to have persist-
ed among the Nations nevertheless.*

Among the Christians, yes. Which goes to show that
the Bible cannot be understood in isolation from the
commentaries.

*In separating the Torah from its Jewish tradition, haven't
the Christians lost sight of its meaning? Isn't Shakespeare's*
Merchant of Venice *a terrible illustration of the sort of falsification of meaning perpetrated by the churches?*

It is our duty to help them to rediscover the meaning.

*The third passage I would like to ask you about is the last
verse of Psalm 137, which is absolutely dreadful. Addressing
the daughter of Babel, the psalmist writes:* Ashrai sheyo'hez
venipets et olalayikh hasala, *"Happy is he who shall seize
your children and dash them against the rock!" Should this
verse be read in the obvious sense, the* pshat, *or in the elicited
sense, the* drash?

What are the Psalms? They are poetry. Now poetry,
by definition, must be interpreted according to the *drash*
and not the *pshat*. Poems are not to be taken literally. In
the simple, simplistic form, this text seems dreadful. But
the poetic passages of the Bible must not be read
literally—that would be a travesty. You know that the

Torah must always be read with the Rashi and the commentaries of the sages.

How do you read the famous passage of Bereshit [Genesis] in which Abraham, speaking privately to the Lord and seeing three bedouins at the entrance to his tent, says: "Lord, if I have deserved Thy favor, do not pass by Thy servant . . . "?

What bothers you about that?

Does it mean that it is more important to welcome passers-by than to talk privately with the Lord? Or, taking it further, that there is more revelation in greeting the stranger—in this case the three bedouins in the desert—than in a dialogue with the Lord?

Abraham is considered a *tzadik*, a Just Man, because the anonymous beggar was more important to him than the visitation of *shekhina*, the presence of God. But by welcoming the poor man or the stranger, we come closer to *shekhina*: it enters along with him.

But is private dialogue with the Lord really a Jewish notion?

Don't forget Moses!

But community prayer seems more important than private prayer in our tradition.

That's true, there is always a neighbor, a relative, a friend. In the end, it is the others who are most important. It is through others, and not by drawing away from them, that we come nearer to God.

The Baba Batra treatise tells how the prophet Elias used to visit a pious man with whom he enjoyed talking. But one day this man had a watchman's shelter built in front of his house, and after that Elias stopped visiting him. I don't understand the moral of this haggada *[talmudic apologue].*

Why not?

I can't see why Elias no longer wanted to visit his friend.

Because of the friend's isolation. The man no longer wanted to see people, and Elias therefore told him: "If you do not want to see other people anymore, then I don't want to see you."

What does the Rashi commentary say? More or less what you do, I think.

I don't recall. I'd better look it up. Before repeating a sage's saying, you have to be sure of its source.

Elie Wiesel gets up to look for the volume containing the Baba Batra treatise of the Babylonian Talmud. As before, he puts on his kipa, *opens the book, and begins to look.*

I don't think the Rashi says anything; perhaps the Tossafot [medieval talmudic commentaries included in all editions along with the Rashi commentary]. Yes, here it is: "It is because once he isolated himself, he could no longer hear the supplications of the poor."

You said solitude . . .

Isolation, not solitude. It's not the same thing. In the Jewish tradition, we have no right to isolate ourselves, to separate ourselves from others.

In rereading the transcripts of our earlier discussions, I realized that two major characters of the Bible went unmentioned in our talk about Evil and exile: Isaac and Job. You seem to have

*written more about Job than about Isaac. Are you more struck
by him than by Isaac?*

The *Akeda* plays a dominant role for me, and if I speak
of it less, that is only because I tried to say everything I
had to say about it in the chapter of *Messengers of God*
devoted to Abraham and Isaac. But their story haunts
me.

Why is the Akeda *called the sacrifice of Abraham and not
the sacrifice of Isaac?*

Actually, *akeda* does not mean "sacrifice" in Hebrew.
That's a mistranslation. The *Akeda* is the story of the
bondage of Isaac. He was not sacrificed. But the real
question is this: why is it referred to as Isaac's ordeal? It
really ought to be called Abraham's ordeal, for that is
what it was: the temptation and punishment of Abraham. I try to answer all these questions in my chapter on
the *Akeda*. But in the Talmud, in the Jewish liturgy, it is
called the Hesed of Abraham, which means the "mercy," or charity, of Abraham. Personally, I prefer to interpret *hesed le Avraham* as meaning: the mercy that was
offered *to* Abraham by God, for it was God who granted
mercy, showing charity to Abraham by not making him
go through with it, by revoking His decree.

But that ignores Isaac's ordeal.

Not at all. In my own way, I speak of Isaac constantly,
in all my writings. In fact, I speak of almost nothing else.
But what I am suggesting is that Abraham's act is often
confused with the virtue of *hesed*. But I ask myself,
where is the *hesed* on Abraham's part, and I can't see
any. There is no charity in him – except in my interpretation, which argues that in fact Abraham was charitable
not so much toward Isaac as toward God. And God, for

His part, was full of *hesed* for Abraham, since in the end
He stopped him. Otherwise, according to the *pshat*,
Abraham would have sacrificed Isaac. In the *drash*, however, the elicited meaning, I think I'm right: Abraham
was trying to make God suffer the ordeal; he was trying
to defy the Lord.

*But could we admit the hypothesis that the entire incident
was nothing more than a contest between Satan and the Lord,
like the story of Job?*

Satan figures in the Talmud's account, but not in the
Bible's. There it is God alone who summons Abraham.
Perhaps God was issuing a challenge to Himself. Job's
story, however, was indeed a contest, a wager between
Satan and God.

*But I still don't understand why our tradition gives primacy
to Abraham's ordeal over Isaac's.*

Because Isaac had no choice. He did not know what
lay in store for him and he could not disobey his father,
whereas Abraham had the choice of obedience or dis
obedience.

*Do you see any link, any similarity, between Abraham's obe-
dience and his climbing of Mount Moriah with Isaac on the one
hand and the journey of all the mothers and fathers to Auschwitz and Treblinka on the other? Even as I speak, I sense that
I have no right to ask such a question, but since I have already
done so, do you have an answer?*

Poetically and symbolically, such a comparison is possible, but I prefer not to make it.

In a short text on the Akeda *recently published in Geneva
under the striking title* Comment taire? *George Steiner*

wrote: "No Jewish father can look upon his son without won-
dering whether he might be ordered to take his life. No Jewish
son can look upon his father without wondering whether he
might be immolated by his own father." Do you share that
scarcely utterable thought?

It's false. "No Jewish father." What does that mean?
"No Jewish son." What an idea! Steiner is often brilliant
and erudite, but he is a bit too quick to exaggerate and
generalize. What does it mean to say "no Jewish father"?
Let him ask around among the three million Jews in New
York, or in France, or in Geneva, where he teaches!

What is the significance of the name Isaac, or Yitzhak: he
who laughs?

In *Messengers of God* I say that Isaac will always
remember the "holocaust" and will be devastated by it to
the end of time, but despite everything, he will still be
capable of laughter. Despite it all, he will laugh.
Laughter comes up in several chapters of Scripture.
Abraham laughs when he fails to understand the word
of God. Sarah laughs when she learns that she will get
pregnant. And finally, Ishmael laughs. I am intrigued by
this metaphysical aspect of laughter.

Somewhere in the Talmud the Hakhamim comment on a
verse in one of the psalms in which it is said that God
laughs. . . .

Yes, but God laughs *with* and not *at* his creatures.

Toward the end of your dialogue with Josy Eisenberg about
Job, you offer a very powerful interpretation of the verse in
which Job says: "Therefore I despise myself and repent in dust
and ashes." You read it not as "I repent," but as "I am consoled."
How do you think he can be consoled by being ashes and dust?

So long as man lives, his life has meaning, even though he is dust and ashes. Whoever understands this transcends his mortal condition. In other words, the meaning he gives his life transcends the ashes, and this can be consoling. Granted, man comes from the earth and to the earth he returns, just as the liturgy says. But during his brief passage, he can sing of the earth, he can work and transform it. That, indeed, is his mission.

When Abraham, pleading for Sodom, says, "dust and ashes that I am," does he prevail over the dust and ashes?

Abraham uses the word *anokhi*, which is not the same as *ani*, the simple "I." *Anokhi* is more or less the sublime I. At that moment Abraham is counterposing his sublime I to the dust and ashes.

In Job ou Dieu dans la tempête *you ask, "Can one pray against God?"' Is that merely a question, or is it already an answer?*

It is a question, but one that contains its own answer.

What is the special greatness of the book of Job, as you see it? Malraux, though an agnostic, called it "the greatest dialogue God and man have ever had."

Malraux said that? Well, some writers love to exaggerate! *The* greatest? Why glorify Job at the expense of Jeremiah or Moses?

But in some sense, isn't the book of Job the first human indictment of God?

It is not an indictment of God. There is no *trial* of God here. Job questions God, but he does not accuse Him.

He never says, "Thou art guilty." He only says, "Thou art responsible," which is not the same thing.

It has occurred to me that of all the masterpieces that sing of human love—of love between man and woman—only the Shir ha-shirim, *the Song of Songs, sings not of hopeless, tragic, and impossible love but of a happiness that goes far beyond the mere joy of encounter and union. This happiness itself bespeaks the greatest love, the only one that is as strong as death. Yet you have never written about the Song of Songs. Why is that?*

The time will come. Solomon wrote only three books: the Song of Songs, Proverbs, and Ecclesiastes. There is a time for everything.

Does that mean that there will come a time when you will speak of it?

Certainly, the day will come that I will speak of Solomon. I will discuss the three phases of his life.

But isn't it remarkable that of all the books on love, the Song of Songs alone sings not of tragic love?

When I think of the *Shir ha-shirim,* I view it in the context of the Bible, not in the context of literature: profane love, courtly love, unhappy love. To me the most important question is, When did Solomon write it? At the beginning or at the end of his life? Some say that it was written when he was young and romantic, others when he was old. Second, why did our sages wait so long before "canonizing" the *Shir ha-shirim*? In the end—fortunately—Rabbi Akiba came along and said: if all the books are holy, the *Shir ha-shirim* is *kodesh kodashim,* the holy of holies. That is what interests me about the *Shir ha-shirim*. And finally, what is the *Shir ha-shirim*? Is it love between one person and another or love between God and Israel or between God and *shekhina*?

I often wonder whether the holy—the kadosh—*is not stronger than the sacred in our tradition. Isn't there a sort of desacralization of nature, for example?*

In any event, the word *kadosh* is not applied to humans, even though the Bible, as we have seen, does say *Kedoshim tihyu*, "You shall be holy."

But doesn't holiness take priority over sacredness?

Everyone seeks the truth and also seeks justice and compassion. But it cannot truly be said that the holy takes priority over the sacred. I could find quotations that attest to the contrary.

Nevertheless, the notion of "holy" contains an inescapable sense of nearness to others, to ethics, which is absent from "sacred."

Indeed. On this point I think you're right.

"Holy" suggests a relation to God that does not exist in the same way in "sacred."

Yes it does. Why not? How can a thing be called sacred without connecting it to a divinity? When it comes to matters like this, we must speak a sentence, fall silent, and then ask ourselves: Is it true? We then realize that it is indeed true, yet at the same time it is not quite true. Because the contrary is equally possible. The beauty of the Talmud is that we can always find an invisible door that suddenly open before us.

On Silence

Philippe de Saint-Cheron: *Your life would suggest that to some extent man is free to choose among the options offered to him, that he is free before the dark forces of existence and of history.*

Elie Wiesel: I certainly believe that. I have to believe it, though I know very well that this belief raises questions. Are we really free? How can we be free? How can we express this freedom when we are conditioned by life and society and are in some sense sustained by God? Once again, it was Rabbi Akiba who said: "Everything is foreordained, yet we are free."

Have you felt this freedom in your own personal life?

You know I don't like to talk about my personal life.

Nevertheless, you did face choices, and you opted for this one or that rather than another.

Of course. But every human being faces choices at one time or another.

But there are destinies, like yours, that are different from others. . . .

We sometimes find ourselves facing paths upon which we cannot refuse to embark; it is as if we were somehow bound in advance. Freedom can be manifested by the duties that are imposed on us.

Did Cain become Cain by choice or despite himself, by the force of circumstance, perhaps because God showed lack of love for him?

I devoted a chapter of *Messengers of God* to him. In one respect I take Cain's side, because God was unfair to him. But I do not defend his crime. He was not fated to kill: he had the power to decide, and he was free to reject that option.

Predestination is in any case not a Jewish notion.

We are free to choose between good and evil, between life and death, between God and idols: it says so in the Torah.

Indifference to the suffering and misery of others, trivialization of violence and death, and pornographic debasement of sexuality are symbolic of our civilization today. What is the meaning of all this meaninglessness?

There is a crisis, of course. But the question I ask myself is this: was the Hurban a reflection of this crisis or its source? In other words, was it both the source of and the reason for this crisis?

But it seems clear that the crisis had already begun before the war.

The theory that the crisis began earlier, festered, and later exploded may have some merit, but the theory that it broke out afterward may also be right.

Might all this meaninglessness be a consequence of the loss of religious faith?

I don't know. I have no answer to that question.

In what way is chaos worse than evil?

In the rabbinical tradition, chaos is always worse than evil. But when do we speak of chaos? When Good and Evil are evenly matched, when the wicked assume the countenance of the Just. That is real chaos.

But isn't chaos also the possibility of . . .

Of anything. Language itself is lost; it becomes a lie, for instinct has no need of language to express itself.

And on a global scale?

The ultimate chaos, obviously, would be the atomic bomb.

At the beginning of our discussions, I asked you about the relation between speech and silence. Do you think that there have been two distinct periods in the holy history of Israel: a time of speech, during the founding events, and a time of silence, since the death of the last prophets? Or is it rather that silence is God's only word?

No, I don't think so at all. We do not know what God *is*, but since He is in everything, it follows that he is in both speech and silence.

But can we speak of two distinct periods: one in which the Lord spoke through His prophets and another in which He is silent?

There is a time of waiting and a time of dénouement, of fulfillment. There was the period of prophecy and the period of the first and second Temples. Those are the proper divisions of time. But the end of prophecy has nothing to do with God's word or His silence. The destruction of the first Temple marked the end of the Prophets, but not the end of the word of God. God continues to speak; it is just that we are neither worthy nor capable of hearing Him. We are not equipped to hear God's voice as the Prophets were. We can no longer grasp His words. The Hurban, I think, is the only period for which we are perhaps entitled to speak of God's silence. But even then, He must have said something. I am convinced that He spoke, though I do not know how. Nor do I know what He said.

A Carmelite priest—Father Jacques, martyr of charity, who was deported (along with Jean Cayrol) to Neue-Gamme and Mauthausen-Güsen for having hidden three Jewish children in his school in Avon—once told a companion in the camp: "Really, if after our deaths it turned out that what we believe is not entirely true, that would be the greatest deception man could suffer."
Do you acknowledge this cry of the religious soul?

I cannot say. Our duty is only to listen to that cry, to hear it again and again, and to heed it with respect and tenderness.

The Talmud reports that at the moment of his death, Rabbi Akiba uttered the words Shma Israel, as so many Jewish martyrs have done throughout history. You have said, however, that according to your Master Saul Liberman, if Rabbi Akiba cried Shma Israel, it was simply because it was the time for that prayer. But you did not say whether you share that interpretation or not.

This was a brilliant discovery on Saul Liberman's part, for the issue here is what attitude to take toward death, in this case the death of a Master. Is death a private matter or not? That is the question posed by tradition. In the Talmud, death is considered the most intimate experience. But at the same time, I know that during the Crusades, during the whirlwinds and pogroms, countless Jews cried Shma Israel as they died. It is the last chance for a Jew to assert his Jewishness. That is the time to say the Shma Israel. If that time is the moment of death, then that is the time to say it. But we have made an example of Rabbi Akiba, because he uttered the first words of the Shma Israel as he died. What was originally a matter of chance, perhaps a coincidence, has therefore gradually become a law.

* * *

Here is a memory that, to my knowledge, Elie Wiesel has recounted only once, during a recent interview (with Brigitte-Fany Cohen, in Elie Wiesel qui êtes-vous?, *Editions de la Manufacture, Lyon, 1987):*

"I pictured myself back in 1945, in the open train that was taking us from Auschwitz to Buchenwald. On the eve of our arrival at the camp, we were completely blanketed by a terrible snowstorm. And suddenly, in the train car, we began shouting 'Shma Israel' —at the wind, the snow, the sky, the whole world. We shouted that 'Shma Israel' at God Himself. At that moment, I felt that this prayer, issued of the Bible, had been awaiting us all that time, preparing to take on a new significance. At that exact instant, a powerful bond was woven between us and the Book."

* * *

Philippe de Saint-Cheron: *I once heard you draw a parallel between Rabbi Akiba and Saul of Tarsus.*

Elie Wiesel: They were contemporaries, yet they never met. How is it that their paths never crossed? Both, I think, aspired to save their fellow men, though in different ways. Where Rabbi Akiba tried to help the Jews from within his own people, Saul of Tarsus tried to "save" them, as he put it, from outside, by taking distance from his people. What divides them is that Rabbi Akiba loved his people absolutely. His prime concern was the unity of the Jewish people, whereas for Saul, it was his conversion.

"For a Jew, there is no deeper fear than the possibility of a schism between ourselves and the God of Israel." You said that during a speech in Paris about Rabbi Hanina ben Teradion. In what sense are we to understand the word "schism"?

In the sense of rupture, separation, divorce. That was the fear in Ezekiel's time, and it persists to this day. Sometimes we wonder whether God has not perhaps deserted us, whether He has not said, "I've had it with you, I will choose another people, another messenger, a scripture other than yours." That is what arouses our anguish.

Wasn't that the cry of the Hebrews in the desert, shortly after they crossed the Red Sea: "Is the Lord still among us?"

At that time, God was still very near. We sometimes find this fear in mystical, especially Hasidic, literature. The people of Israel say to God: "In the beginning we were young and beautiful, but now we are old. Remember that there was once a time – the time of our betrothal, of our marriage on Sinai – when the Knesset Israel, the Assembly of Israel, was beautiful! Now it is no longer so, but may You still remember!" Once again, this is fear of divorce, of estrangement: "Do not divorce us; do not draw away from us!"

*But isn't there a kind of grave beauty in this fear that the
Lord might draw away from His people?*

I don't know whether there is beauty in the fear of divorce, but certainly there is anxiety, anguish; and this
anguish, of course, can generate a rediscovery of God,
thus bringing us nearer to Him.

*It reminds me of the passage in the Talmud where it is writ-
ten that Adonoi weeps whenever a man and a woman divorce.*

Yes, every time a couple gets divorced, God weeps.

*On Simchas Torah, for the first time in my life I understood
what it meant to dance with the Sefer Torah. On that day I
realized that to a Jew, the dance on Simchas Torah is as fundamental as the fast on Tisha b'Ab or Yom Kippur.*

That's true. Judaism is a whole, a totality of expres-
sions and experiences. It may seem surprising that on
Tisha b'Ab we remember redemption and on the day of
a wedding we remember the destruction of the Temple.
We weep and laugh at the same time. But on Simchas
Torah there is only joy. There is another element in the
Simchas Torah festival too, however: it is the day on
which the cycle of weekly readings of the Torah is
closed, whereupon it begins anew. We complete it and
then immediately start again with Bereshit [Genesis].

How far back does dance go in the Jewish liturgy?

It goes back to antiquity, but I think that in those days
the dance took place on Yom Kippur and not on Simchas
Torah. The change was made later, because all the congregations of Israel journeyed to Jerusalem on Shemini
Atzeret. That solemn occasion marked the third pil-
grimage of the year, during which they sang and

danced. The weekly reading of the Torah as we know it
today began only with Ezra, who incorporated it into the
liturgy after the first destruction of the Temple.

Does Hasidism attribute great importance to dance?

The Hasidim dance a lot.

*Does dance have what might be called a theological sig-
nificance in Judaism?*

The Hasidic teachers believed in dance, and some of
them raised it to a theological virtue, notably Rabbi
Moshe-Leib of Sassov and the famous "Grandfather of
Shpolai."

*Does the ritual rocking back and forth of Jews at prayer have
some relation to dance?*

It has various meanings, of course, but most of all it
permits the attainment of ecstasy.

But ecstasy can also be attained through dance.

Certainly, except that it would be more difficult to
pray while dancing. But we do sing as we dance.

*Now I would like to move from Simchas Torah to Yom Kip-
pur. On the day of atonement, every Jew accepts blame both for
his own sins and for those that he himself has not committed.
What is the meaning of this deliberate acceptance of guilt for
crimes or infractions that we have not personally committed?*

Though we are responsible first for others and secondly for ourselves, we must nonetheless accept blame
for our own sins first. Why is that? If I know someone
who has sinned and I let it happen, then I am myself at

fault. What is sin, after all? It is an expression of misfortune, and if I was not present at the time of this misfortune, I thereby allowed the man or woman in question to commit an infraction. Hence my responsibility.

But that kind of responsibility is limitless. Someone might very well commit a crime in which I was not involved, yet I must act as though I was, as though I bore my share of the responsibility.

It is as if each of us were involved in the misfortune of others. But in a certain sense, it is easily said. We will be forgiven. And since we know that we will be forgiven, we lay out before God even the impossible and unthinkable things. But this shows that our relation to others is so all-encompassing as to make us blame ourselves for their sins.

Do you think that death acquires meaning even in its absurdity and meaninglessness? In other words, does death have a transcendent meaning? Can we speak of a transcendence in death?

Who am I to answer such a question?

In the Jewish tradition, I believe, our Masters, the Hakhamim, say that the grave is not a refuge. Does this mean that there is something in death that goes beyond it, something like a responsibility from which even death does not release us?

This is such a weighty, serious question that it would be irresponsible of me to try to answer it without spending weeks and months thinking about it.

But this principle of our tradition, that the grave is not a refuge, would seem to suggest that death is not the end of everything. With my death . . .

Of course it means that there is another life. We find this notion, however, not in biblical but in rabbinical thought. *Hasharat ha-naiphesh*. The one is as important as the other, except that it takes much longer to read and study rabbinical thought.

Doesn't Judaism perceive the mystery of death as the instant at which a human being is deprived of the Torah, when the Torah departs as if into exile?

It is not death; it is exile.

There is a talmudic apologue in which our Masters compare and contrast the moment at which the Torah is taken from a dying person with the moment at which it was given on Mount Sinai. The Torah that is given and the Torah that is taken away are thereby joined.

Perhaps. The Torah is life. Without the Torah there is no life. That is a symbolic statement. But when you say "death," you're talking about something that is not merely symbolic but on the contrary very concrete. Death is when there is no more of me, when a person no longer exists and can no longer help, speak, sympathize, or love.

But may we believe in a spiritual presence which, even after death, remains among the people a cherished human being has loved?

Really, we are getting into things that must not be spoken of aloud.

* * *

We are running out of time. With time pressing, I begin asking questions as they occur to me, for once asked, they will not go unanswered. But if there is no final question, still less can there be a final answer.

*   *   *

What is it that is most radically counterposed to the mystery of death and the mystery of Evil?

The mysteries of life and of Good.

Do you ever regret having begun to talk about the Hurban in the first place, thus breaking a silence of centuries?

Yes, sometimes I do regret it, because I believe that in the end the word was not heeded. Some people think they know but do not, perhaps because the word could not be heeded. I often wonder about that. The witness has spoken, but his testimony has not been heard. Then I come to doubt the nature, vocation, and mission of speech itself. If the testimony had been heard, then things that are happening today would not be happening: the hatred, anti-Semitism, hunger, torture, and humiliation that so many human beings are inflicting on so many others.

And in another domain, the revisionists . . .

Are doing all they can to lie.

Considering the works of Paul Celan, Nelly Sachs, Penderecki, and your own Ani Maamin *cantata, do you believe that poetry and music can go further than literature in communicating the incommunicable?*

Perhaps, but everything is literature. Music is language too, as is poetry. Even painting is language, in the most noble and tragic sense of the word. It is language asking hard questions of itself. Questions can be asked musically too. Through music a composer can cause himself pain and can seek to grasp the essence of that pain. The real question is this: can the incommunicable be communicated? I do not believe that the experience we had is communicable, yet we strive to communicate it nevertheless.

Have you heard Krystof Penderecki's Auschwitz Oratorio?

Yes, I have. It is stirring, sometimes quite moving.

I would like to return to the Barbie trial for a moment. Two Catholics — Joseph Rovant and Jacques Sommet — took positions different from yours. The former was against the trial, while the latter was amenable to a pardon for Barbie.

I don't know them, and I don't know why they said what they did. I have no idea what their real, underlying motivation was. All this is so personal. In the end, every person must take his own stand on this mystery and on the fear it arouses. Some will say that they will never forget. Others that we must forget. Still others that we must forgive, even knowing that to forgive and to forget go hand in hand, that one comes with the other. So let's not generalize. Every case is individual.

What is your favorite Hasidic legend or story?

They are all my favorites. To choose one would be to deny the others, and I love them all.

Isn't there one in particular that might speak to all we've said about Evil and Exile?

I think you might find one like that by Rabbi Nahman of Bratzlav, with his mendicants, or by Rabbi Moshe-

Leib of Sassov, about dance—both of whom we have talked about—or by Rabbi Levi-Yitzhak of Berdichev, with his protest against God's silence. The stories remain open, you see, in each Hasidic life and each Hasidic destiny. Rabbi Moshe-Leib of Sassov once said, "If you want the spark, seek it in the ashes."

What do you think of Adorno's terrible comment, "After Auschwitz there can be no poetry"?

I understand it. How can we continue to sing, after Auschwitz? How can we put words together, when the murderers used the same words, perhaps in the same way, to cause such ruin, catastrophe, and agony?

Yet people wrote poems even in the Camps.

That's right. In Auschwitz we had the wrenching poetry of the dying, and prayers were said for the dead. I therefore prefer to interpret Adorno's remark, like similar statements by other people, as a question. It is better if we end the phrase with a question mark: Can poetry still be written after Auschwitz?

There is something that still troubles me about the nature of Evil: does Evil exist in itself, as a positive phenomenon, or should it rather be seen as the negative pole of Good? Isn't Evil the negation of kindness and love? Have we really talked about Evil as such, or on the contrary as that which stands opposed to Good?

We have talked about war, hunger, shame, torture. This is more than the mere absence of Good. It is Evil.

Evil is not passive, but active. It is self-assertive, and it strives to conquer. If it is not halted, if it is not vanquished, it can triumph, just as desert can triumph over fertile land, or the sea over a sandy beach.

Then Evil exists independent of its negative relation to love and to good?

In human terms, certainly. The reason the Nazis were filled with hate was not because they did not know love. In all probability, they did love. Yet they hated too.

Hatred was their very nature.

Unfortunately. I remember that when I saw Eichmann in his glass cage, I was frightened, even though he was powerless. But he was still frightening, because he was Evil itself, and Evil is always frightening.

Do you find that living among four languages—English, French, Hebrew, and Yiddish—affords you a link between worlds?

My generation spoke various languages. We were born in countries in which nationalities, religions, and traditions were intermingled. The Christians spoke Yiddish as fluently as we did. At home in Sighet we spoke Romanian, Hungarian, German, Yiddish of course, Czech, Russian, and Ukrainian—and Hebrew on the Sabbath. Of all these languages, today I have retained only four or five, apart from French and English.

But doesn't it provide a shortcut in time, history, or memory?

I seek no shortcuts.

* * *

"I seek no shortcuts . . ."
As I was walking up Park Avenue a few minutes after leaving Elie Wiesel's, a building on the corner caught my eye: the

Park Avenue Synagogue. To the left of the entrance, an inscription was carved in stone.

Lish'moa ainkat assir.
Hear the cry of the oppressed.
Psalm 102, 21

Epilogue

One last image of Elie Wiesel. On January 17, 1988, the day before a meeting of seventy-five Nobel Prize winners in Paris, Elie Wiesel insisted on going to Auschwitz-Birkenau. It was on January 18, 1945, that he and his father had left the camp, transferred to Buchenwald. Lech Walesa, who had been unable to come to Paris, waited for him at the Cracow airport. Though they had never met, on television their encounter looked like a true reunion. Wiesel and Walesa embraced at the airport, and they did so again at the wall of death in Auschwitz, after the *kaddish* was said.

"A man like you is proof that we can change things," Elie Wiesel said to Lech Walesa, who replied, "I knew you would come; a man like you can do anything." There was pathos in their walk through the camp, and in their common prayer. Wiesel, his expression strained, and Walesa, his face grave, were united in a like suffering, a like communion. The Auschwitz survivor wore a Solidarity badge, and had his arm around the shoulder of the founder of the Polish trade union. Walesa and Wiesel: two symbols of the fight for human rights. A unique and stirring meeting of two Nobel Peace Prize winners in the land of Poland, strewn with the ashes of millions of Jews. The presence of the dead and the fight for the living were brought together in our memories by the moving words spoken by the two men at the Memorial of the Martyr of the Nations in Birkenau—

alongside the ruins of the gas chambers, at the end of the "ramp to nowhere" which the young Eliezer had walked forty-four years before. "I thought that Auschwitz was the end of the world," Elie Wiesel said. "Now I realize how important it is to rebuild." And Lech Walesa replied: "This morning, at your side, I came to understand many things. I will return often to Auschwitz."